For Patricia
New Year's Day 1979

John

The Indian Legacy of Charles Bird King

THE INDIAN LEGACY
OF CHARLES BIRD KING

Herman J. Viola

Copublished by Smithsonian Institution Press
and Doubleday & Company, Inc.

Copyright © 1976 by Herman J. Viola   All rights reserved
First edition
Designed by Elizabeth A. Sur
Printed in the United States of America by Eastern Press, Inc.
Smithsonian Institution Press, Washington, D.C. 20560
ISBN 0-87474-943-3
Doubleday & Company, Inc., New York 10017
ISBN 0-385-12485-6

Library of Congress Cataloging in Publication Data
Viola, Herman J.
‘The Indian legacy of Charles Bird King.
(Smithsonian Institution Press publication; no. 6256)
“Catalog of War Department Indian Gallery”: p.
Bibliography: p.
Includes index.
1. King, Charles Bird, 1785-1862. 2. Indians of
North America—Portraits. 3. Indians of North America—
Government relations—1789-1869. I. Title.
ND237.K53V56   759.13   76-15022

Jacket: Nesouaquoit [Bear in the Fork of a Tree], Fox, by
Charles Bird King. Sotheby Parke Bernet Inc., New York.

Cover: James Monroe peace medal.

Frontispiece: Charles Bird King. Mrs. Walter Harvey.

To Susan

Contents

Preface

Publication of *The Indian Legacy of Charles Bird King* fulfills a cherished hope held for more than a decade. I first became acquainted with King's remarkable series of portraits through my work on Thomas L. McKenney, the good-hearted but sometimes overzealous founder of the Bureau of Indian Affairs. As my research on McKenney progressed, the story of Charles Bird King and the War Department gallery of Indian portraits began to unfold. I became convinced the story deserved to be told. Although McKenney conceived the idea of painting the portraits of Indian leaders invited to Washington, King made it possible. This kindly artist from Rhode Island may not have been as gifted as George Catlin, Karl Bodmer, and the others of his day who painted portraits of the Native Americans, but his work was important and he deserves recognition. I hope this book does credit to his art and his subjects.

A grant from the Penrose Fund of the American Philosophical Society greatly facilitated my research for this book. This grant enabled me to collect on a systematic basis copies of the King Indian portraits.

Portions of this book appeared previously in *The Smithsonian Journal of History* (1968), *The American Scene* (1970), *The American West* (1972), and *Thomas L. McKenney, Architect of America's Early Indian Policy* (1974).

All writers must acknowledge their reliance on others, and I am in debt to many. Thanks are especially due to my colleagues in the Anthropology Department of the Smithsonian Institution, John C. Ewers and William C. Sturtevant. Despite their own long-standing interest in King and his Indian portraits, they encouraged me to write this book.

Thanks are also due to the Gulf States Paper Corporation staff, especially to Jack Warner, James Montgomery, and Doris Fletcher. They have followed my work on King closely and provided generous access to their large and significant collection of his portraits.

DuVal Radford of Bedford, Virginia, Thornton Boileau of Birmingham, Michigan, and Lawrence G. Claggett of Easton, Maryland, graciously granted permission to use copies of their paintings in this book.

I am particularly grateful to Bayard LeRoy King of Saunderstown, Rhode Island, who discovered the original King charcoal sketches and permitted me to be the first to publish them.

Two individuals I most wanted to enjoy this book passed away before it was completed: John and Maria McKenney of Centerville, Maryland, enthusiastically supported my work on their illustrious ancestor and the Indian gallery.

I want to thank the staff of the Smithsonian Institution Press, especially Maureen Jacoby, Stephen Kraft, Felix Lowe, Hope Pantell, and Elizabeth Sur.

Others who also deserve mention for helping me with this book are Samella Anderson, Whitfield Bell, Kathleen Collier, Andrew Cosentino, Richard Crawford, Ralph Ehrenberg, Robert Fowler, Herman Friis, Clifford Evans, Monroe Fabian, Rolf Gilberg, Deborah Harsch, Marilyn Harsch, Edward E. Hill, Karen Holman, David Hunt, Arild Hridtfeldt, Sara Jackson, Marie Jones, Porter Kier, Margaret Klapthor, Victor Krantz, Robert Kvasnicka, Beatrice Menchaca, Betty C. Monkman, Michael Musick, Frederick Pernell, George Perros, George Phebus, Francis Paul Prucha, S.J., Paula Richardson, Murphy Smith, Charles South, William Truettner, Victoria Washington, and Lloyd Wineland.

The staffs and collections of numerous libraries and manuscript repositories have served me well. As an archivist, I know only too well the burdens imposed by pesky researchers like me. I wish to acknowledge specifically my debts to the following: the National Anthropological Archives and National Collection of Fine Arts of the Smithsonian Institution, the National Archives and Records Service, the Library of Congress, the Thomas Gilcrease Institute of American History and Art, the Massachusetts Historical Society, the Houghton Library and the Peabody Museum of Archaeology and Ethnology at Harvard University, the New-York Historical Society, the New York Public Library, the Historical Society of Pennsylvania, the American Philosophical Society, the Danish National Museum, the Corcoran Gallery of Art, the Chicago Historical Society, the Joslyn Art Museum, the Cherokee National Historical Society, the Albright-Knox Art Gallery, the Nebraska State Historical Society, the Buffalo and Erie County Historical Society, the White House Historical Association, and the Wilmette Historical Commission.

Special thanks are due to the staff of the Redwood Library and Athenaeum, especially Donald T. Gibbs and Richard L. Champlin. They have continually provided invaluable assistance during my decade-long research for this book.

I especially appreciate the considerable editorial assistance of Jan Shelton Danis, who also prepared the index.

To my wife Susan must go the final and most important thanks. As happened to so many wives in American history, her husband was "captured" by Indians. Only I can fully appreciate her uncomplaining sacrifice of countless weekends, holidays, and evenings so I could work on King, McKenney, and the War Department gallery.

Introduction

One of the earliest and most persistent themes in American art has been the pictorial interpretation of the native peoples of the New World. Before the first permanent English settlements were founded in Virginia and Massachusetts a few firsthand observers of Indians on the East Coast of North America pictured life among the Indians they met. These artists' works, conveyed to the peoples of England and Western Europe in the form of widely circulated engravings, helped to satisfy widespread curiosity about the general appearance and lifeways of the native peoples in the remote and newly discovered American wilderness—how they dressed; how they built their homes and laid out and fortified their villages; how they gained subsistence by hunting, fishing, and cultivating food crops; how they warred on their enemies; conducted their sacred ceremonies; and even how they cared for their dead.

Jacques Le Moyne de Morgues among the Timucuas of northern Florida in 1564, John White among the Siouan tribes of coastal North Carolina (then known as part of Virginia) in 1585, and Samuel de Champlain among the Huron Indians and their neighbors on the St. Lawrence River during the first decade of the seventeenth century produced graphic records of aboriginal life and customs of lasting value to students of history and anthropology, although the works of both of the French artists are known today almost entirely through engraved reproductions of the originals. Even so, and valuable as these works are as cultural documents, they are deficient as records of the physical appearance of the Indians. Those early artists were not portraitists, and the small faces on their full-figured renderings of Indians lack precise, detailed definition of individuality.

The individual Indian began to emerge as a subject for portraiture when leaders of powerful Indian tribes whose allegiance the English coveted were escorted across the Atlantic to visit London, the seat of English colonial power, to meet the ruling monarch and to be impressed by the wonders of English civilization. Then and there, and as a record of these Indians' visits, professional portraitists—men carefully trained to observe and to record the subtleties of facial proportions and contours that define a sitter's individual likeness—drew or painted these prominent Indians.

Although an unnamed English artist painted Pocahontas as early as 1616, it was not until the early years of the eighteenth century that a series of portraits of Indian visitors to London appeared. Jan Verelst, a London-based, Flemish portraitist, executed full-length portraits of four Iroquois sachems brought to England in 1710 to meet Queen Anne and to strengthen their ties with the English in their competition with the French in the American wilderness. Numerous other chiefs of both northern and southern woodland tribes visited the seat of British power in London and were pictured by artists prior to the Revolutionary War. As early as 1734 Willem Verelst painted a remarkably realistic portrait of the powerful Creek chief Tomachichi and his nephew during their visit to London. Not only did this painting strongly define the facial features of both man and boy but it also revealed a striking family resemblance between the two.

Probably the first really successful Indian portraits painted from life within the present United States were those of two Delaware chiefs, Lapowinsa and Tish-cohan, executed in 1735 by the Swedish-born artist Gustavus Hesselius. He referred to himself as a "face painter," a humble title to which the earlier delineators of Indians in America could not aspire. These portraits were ordered by John Penn, the Pennsylvania Proprietor, who two years later negotiated the unsavory Walking Treaty with the Delawares.

In many respects the United States followed English colonial precedent in Indian affairs. Not only did the United States continue to negotiate treaties with the various Indian tribes as if they were independent nations but the secretary of war, who was responsible for the conduct of Indian affairs in the new nation, brought delegations of Indian chiefs to the seat of the national government to impress them with both the power and the friendship of the United States and to strengthen alliances with their tribes.

The English custom of portraying such chiefly visitors to the seat of government also persisted—at first on a sporadic and unofficial basis, and later as a matter of government policy. As early as 1790 the famed "artist of the American Revolution," John Trumbull, happened to be in our temporary capital city of New York when a delegation of Creek Indians from the piny woods came there to meet President Washington and to sign their tribe's first treaty with the United States on August 7, 1790. Trumbull was impressed by these Indian leaders' "dignity of manner, form, countenance and expression, worthy of Roman senators." Even though they refused to pose for him because they regarded his art as magic, Trumbull managed "by stealth" to draw striking pencil portraits of several of these chiefs, some clad in military uniforms given them by the government.

The capital had been established in Washington when Thomas Jefferson welcomed the first delegation of Indians from the newly acquired Louisiana Territory in the spring of 1804. They were the first Indians from the Great Plains to visit Washington, Osage Indians, whom the president looked upon as "the great nation South of the Missouri, as the Sioux are great North of that river. With these two powerful nations we must stand well, because in their quarter we are miserably weak."

While they were in the East, a refugee French artist, Charles B.J.F. de Saint-Mémin, secured excellent likenesses of their head chief, White Hair, and several other members of the delegation with the aid of a mechanical device known as a physiognotrace with which he traced the exact outlines of their profiles. Even though Meriwether Lewis purchased some of Saint-Mémin's Indian portraits to illustrate his planned report of the Lewis and Clark explorations—a report he never completed because of his untimely murder —artists' initiative rather than government sponsorship appears to have accounted for the portraits of Indian visitors to New York, Philadelphia, and Washington executed during the early decades of our national life.

It was Thomas McKenney, United States superintendent of Indian trade in Georgetown, then port of entry for the District of Columbia, who conceived the idea of developing a government collection of portraits of prominent Indians who visited Washington. The first group of Indians to be so memorialized were members of a very picturesque delegation from beyond the Mississippi who were brought to Washington in 1821 during James Monroe's administration. McKenney engaged the services of Charles Bird King, a well-known Washington portraitist, who had studied under the great Benjamin West and others, to paint this series of portraits.

After McKenney took charge of the Bureau of Indian Affairs in the War Department in 1824, he took vigorous steps to enlarge the government's collection of Indian portraits which was hung in his offices. In 1832 Secretary of War James Barbour stated that he approved McKenney's plan for "preserving the likenesses of some of the most distinguished among this most extraordinary race of people" because he believed "that this race was about to become extinct, and that a faithful resemblance of the most remarkable among them would be full of interest in after-times."

There was no dearth of Indian delegations trekking into Washington during the decades of the 1820s and 1830s. This was a very active period of governmental negotiations with numerous Indian tribes. The frontier of settlement was moving rapidly westward and Congress decreed the removal of many woodland tribes to lands west of the Mississippi to make way for white settlers. Numerous treaties were made with both the migrating eastern tribes and those farther west who ceded lands on which to locate the migrants from the East. No fewer than eighteen treaties were signed in the city of Washington between 1824 and 1838. Each signing was attended by a delegation of chiefs and headmen of the tribe or tribes concerned. Other tribes sent delegations to Washington to discuss land cessions which were later formally negotiated in the field.

At times there were so many Indian chiefs in Washington that King alone could not paint all their portraits. At such times he called upon his friend and pupil, George Cooke, to paint likenesses of some of them. Yet King alone, during the years 1821 to 1842 painted some one hundred Indian visitors to Washington, and he also copied for the government collection some twenty-six other Indian portraits from life by the less able artist James Otto Lewis, painted at treaty councils in the field and in the Indian country.

King painted from life Indian leaders of at least twenty tribes—Cherokee, Choctaw, Creek, Seminole, and Yuchi leaders from the South; Ojibwas, Potawatomis, Menominees, Sac, Fox, and Senecas from the Great Lakes region; Iowas, Kansas, Omahas, Otos, and Pawnees from the central Great Plains; Eastern, Yankton, and Yanktonai Dakotas, and a lone Assiniboin from far up the Missouri River. At that time the United States had not yet developed relations with some of the tribes of the western high plains and the Rocky Mountains. Texas had not yet joined the Union, and the United States had not yet acquired the Mexican cession.

No artist of King's time or earlier pictured Indian leaders of more different tribes, with the single exception of George Catlin, who traveled widely in the Indian country beyond the frontiers of white settlement to paint likenesses of leaders of more than forty tribes. Although in his travels Catlin met Indians of lower status, he too preferred to picture prominent chiefs and members of their families. They owned the finest costumes and cut the finest figures in their dress clothing. Catlin, too, was driven by a common motivation to picture Indians for posterity. He believed their picturesque cultures were disappearing before the advance of white settlement and the exposure of Indians to white men's wars, diseases, and vices.

Actually, King began to paint Plains Indians as visitors to Washington nearly a decade before Catlin went west to picture them in their own country. King probably was the first white artist to paint an Indian wearing a flowing-feather bonnet of eagle feathers. He was the first to paint Plains Indian women. They were the attractive young wives of Iowa and Oto chiefs who accompanied their husbands to the Great Father's village on the Potomac. Some of King's Indian subjects were leaders of national prominence, such as Keokuk, Black Hawk, and Red Jacket, and were painted by other artists. Others were chiefs of importance in the history of individual states or regions. Many of them are not known to have been pictured by other artists.

A comparison of King's lone Assiniboin portrait with Catlin's portrait of the same man executed a few months earlier, and of his portrait of the Pawnee hero Petalesharro, with one of that Indian by the Philadelphia artist John Neagle, suggests that King may not always have been successful in obtaining a likeness of his Indian sitters. On the other hand, the fact that he was called upon to make smaller-scale replicas for his Indian sitters to take home with them seems to indicate that they appreciated his portraiture.

The loss of the great majority of King's original Indian portraits in the fire that swept the art gallery in the Smithsonian "castle" on January 24, 1865, is mitigated to a considerable degree by the fact that these portraits were handsomely reproduced as large, full-color lithographs in Thomas McKenney and James Hall's three-volume classic, *History of the Indian Tribes of North America,* a quarter of a century earlier, and by the fact that King painted replicas of a number of his most important Indian portraits for himself and for private collectors. Many of these replicas survive, and are well reproduced in this book.

John C. Ewers

The Artist and the Superintendent

"This great gallery [is] . . . like wine, the longer it is kept, the better. The further off we get from the Indians, & they from us, the greater interest all the public [will] feel in them."[1] This was written in 1833 about more than one hundred portraits of American Indians then hanging like troops in formation in even rows on every bit of available wall space of a cramped War Department office in Washington, D.C. Faces in war paint peered from behind doors, feathered headdresses stuck up over cupboards, figures wrapped in buffalo robes hung between windows. Known as the "Indian Gallery," this impressive array was primarily the work of one man, Charles Bird King, a talented Washington artist who only now is receiving recognition for his important role in recording for posterity the physical appearances and picturesque costumes of the Native Americans in the era before photography.

Charles Bird King's personal life is largely unrecorded.[2] He was a bachelor, a man of exemplary character and simple tastes. Frugality was a dominant attribute, and he acquired considerable wealth in his long and productive life. By heritage, he should have been a soldier, not an artist. For at least four generations, one or more members of the King family had entered military service, but he broke with this tradition.

The artist was born in Newport, Rhode Island, in 1785, the only child of Deborah Bird of Newport and Captain Zebulon King, an infantry officer from Massachusetts who had served with distinction in the American Revolution. Like so many other veterans of the Revolution, Zebulon King went west after the war. He may have intended to speculate in lands, perhaps only to claim the 300 acres the federal government had awarded him for his war service. In any case, on May 1, 1790, he was killed and scalped by Indians near Marietta, Ohio.[3] His son was only four years old at the time. Deborah King never remarried but chose instead to live with her widowed mother in Newport. There her son's interest in art was encouraged by some of the leading craftsmen of the city, including the artisan-artist Samuel King.

Charles Bird King lived in Newport a relatively short time. By 1800, at the age of fifteen, the obviously gifted young man was in New York City receiving his first formal art instruction from the portraitist Edward Savage. Five years later he was in London studying under Benjamin West in the Royal Academy. King spent seven years in London and roomed for a time with Thomas Sully, later the leading portrait painter of Philadelphia. Returning to the United States in 1812 because of the war with England, King spent the next several years as an itinerant artist. He worked in Philadelphia, then in Baltimore and Richmond, before settling permanently in the District of Columbia. King shrewdly realized that a competent portrait painter could anticipate a flourishing business from the politically and

Mrs. John Quincy Adams, by Charles Bird King. National Collection of Fine Arts, Smithsonian Institution.

socially ambitious residents of the fledgling capital being carved out of inhospitable marshlands at the confluence of the Potomac and Anacostia rivers.

Indeed, the city's economic potential was the main attraction for King, because Washington in 1819 had little else to offer. The city had been the seat of government less than two decades and reflected its youth. Pavement was nonexistent; streets were dust bowls or quagmires, depending on the weather. Mosquitoes thrived in the marshy ground, while hogs rooted in garbage-strewn roadways. Nevertheless, an air of optimism about the capital's future prevailed, perhaps inspired by the government's massive rebuilding program necessitated by the destruction of the public buildings by the British during the War of 1812. A cluster of four identical federal office buildings was nearing completion next to the recently rebuilt White House, while at the opposite end of Pennsylvania Avenue a glistening Capitol building once again dominated the Washington skyline. Certainly, King was not alone in his decision to make the nation's capital his home; the rapidly growing city already boasted a population of close to twenty thousand as the bright prospects of the federal government attracted ambitious and energetic young people like the artist from Rhode Island.

King had no difficulty adjusting to life in the capital. Gracious and courtly, he made friends easily and was readily accepted into Washington's first circles. He soon established a patronage few artists of his day could match. Among the political giants of the early nineteenth century who commissioned his services were James Monroe, Henry Clay, John Quincy Adams, and John C. Calhoun. Perhaps King's ready wit and ability to converse freely on many subjects, which helped to relieve the tedium of sitting for a portrait, appealed to them as much as his artistic skill. Not all his patrons found the conversation to their liking, however. Mrs. John Quincy Adams, who sat for her portrait shortly after King moved to Washington, scolded the artist for "treating religious topics with . . . levity and disrespect." As the indignant Louisa Adams later reported, "I took the liberty of telling him he had better confine himself to subjects which he understood." Her husband, on the other hand, had few complaints. "He is one of the best portrait painters in the country; little inferior to [Gilbert?] Stewart," the normally caustic Adams noted in his diary. "He is also an ingenious, thinking man, with a faculty of conversing upon almost any topic."[4]

King built a studio and gallery on the east side of Twelfth Street between E and F streets, but in fine weather he preferred to work under a bower of trees in the garden.

A lover of art and antiques, King soon had his home and studio bulging with bric-a-brac and a large and valuable art collection. King was also very fond of children. He always had a coin or two for those he met while strolling about the streets of Washington, and he took special delight in inviting groups of children into his cluttered studio where he regaled them with toys and sweets while they poked into all the nooks and crannies.

As King grew older, he became increasingly absent-minded, much to the amusement of his friends, who delighted in relating anecdotes about his forgetfulness. Typical is the story told by Joseph Shillington, a Washington book dealer. King went to the bookshop one day and urged his friend to visit his gallery, of which he was justifiably proud. Shillington agreed and spent a pleasant half-hour or so browsing among the paintings; but when he tried to leave, he found the door locked and King gone. The artist had forgotten his friend was in the studio and had gone for a walk, leaving poor Shillington to escape through a rear window.[5]

King had not been in Washington more than a few months when he met Thomas Loraine McKenney. The friendship was to have a profound influence on the artist's career. Author, administrator, humanitarian, McKenney was a key figure in the nation's Indian affairs in the first quarter of the nineteenth century. As superintendent of Indian trade, he administered the network of government trading houses for the Indians known as the factory system. In 1824 he became the first head of the Bureau of Indian Affairs, serving with distinction until 1830, when he was dismissed during President Andrew Jackson's general house cleaning. While in public office, McKenney was the major architect of two government programs that had tremendous impact on the Native Americans in this period. Largely through his efforts, Congress in 1819 passed the Indian Civilization Act, which provided $10,000 annually for the support of schools in the Indian country, and in 1830 it passed the Indian Removal Act, which provided for the resettlement of eastern tribes west of the Mississippi River. He also founded the first museum in Washington, which he called "The Archives of the American Indian."[6]

McKenney, who liked to be called "Colonel," began the archives soon after he became superintendent of Indian trade in 1816, housing it in a three-story, red brick building that still stands on M Street adjacent to the City Tavern in the heart of Georgetown. As he later explained, McKenney deplored the lack of an archives "in which might have been enrolled the progress of things relating to our aborigines." Not only would such an archives

Opposite: Left, Thomas L. McKenney, 1836, by Harrison Gray Otis. Lawrence Claggett. ■ Right, Office of Indian Trade building in Washington, D.C., as it looked in 1976. Built in 1796 as the Bank of Columbia, the building at 3212 M Street, N. W., served as headquarters for the factory system from 1807 to 1822. The structure was converted into a firehouse in 1883, when the two large doors were cut into the facade. In 1972 Congress authorized restoration of the building as the National Firefighting Museum and Center for Fire Prevention. Charles Photographers.

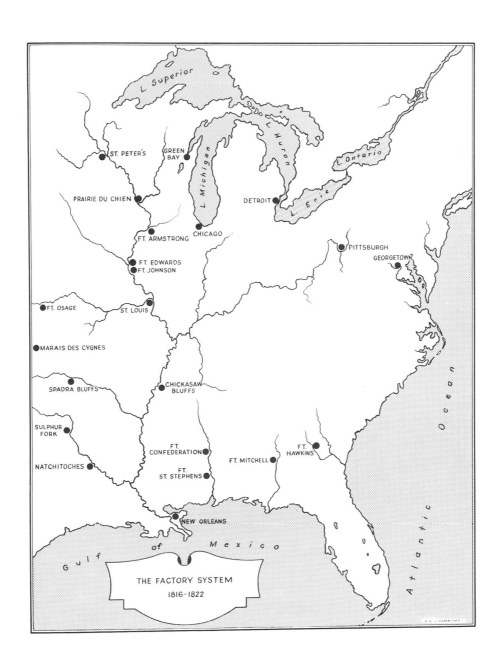

THE FACTORY SYSTEM
1816-1822

be an invaluable aid for the administration of Indian affairs, he reasoned, but it also could be "preserved . . . for the inspection of the curious, and the information of future generations."[7] Convinced that the Indians would disappear through assimilation into American society, McKenney spent considerable time, energy, and funds during his government career collecting everything he could find about them. What he established bore little similarity to a modern archives, however, but resembled rather an ethnological museum.

Apparently, the first items in the archives were some "Indian implements" he received from the secretary of war in the summer of 1817. The next day McKenney sent a circular to his eight factors, who had charge of the trading houses, calling their attention "to a subject which if it will serve no other end [will] gratify my individual curiosity." The circular authorized each factor to barter as much as a hundred dollars worth of trade goods to obtain curiosities peculiar to the tribes trading at his post. Besides bows, arrows, and clothing, McKenney welcomed any "natural curiosity whether of minerals, or animals, or plants."[8]

The circular met with a favorable response. At least four of the factors sent specimens to the Indian office, although the most conscientious collector was John Johnson of Prairie du Chien. Between 1817 and 1822, when the factory system was abolished, Johnson forwarded three barrels of curiosities for which he had traded $319.60 worth of factory merchandise. The factor had not been very discriminating, however. As McKenney informed him in 1820, "I have received a superabundance of Otter Skins & Moccasins." On the other hand, McKenney had "no Bows—two or three good Bows, & quivers, I should like to have, or indeed any thing that shall not be like those already procured." He especially wanted "a few scalps," if they could be obtained without letting the Indians think they were desirable. McKenney suggested that Johnson tell the owners that scalps were "disgraceful appendages & ought to be sent away, as indicating a practice which is growing abhorrant even amongst Indians."[9] McKenney received no scalps, but he did assemble a worthy collection of artifacts, manuscripts, and books relating to the American Indian.

The arrival of Charles Bird King on the Washington scene inspired the imaginative McKenney to add portraits to his archives. Visiting the artist in his studio, McKenney outlined his rather unusual proposal. Would King paint portraits of American Indians for the federal government? The superintendent promised a steady flow of subjects from the numerous Indian delegations that trooped through Washington each year on business. Since he had the responsibility of caring for them while they were in the capital, McKenney could easily arrange their visits to the studio. King needed little persuading. It was an ideal opportunity for an aspiring artist anxious to get established. Payment was guaranteed; the Indians, few of whom could even speak English, were unlikely to complain about his work or conversation; and, since the delegations were normally in Washington for several weeks at a time, the sittings could be scheduled at the artist's convenience.

Thus began King's long and profitable association with the Indian office. For twenty years, the bureau regularly commissioned him to paint portraits of prominent Indian leaders who visited Washington. He charged the government $20 for busts and $27 for full figures, although in certain instances his fee was substantially higher. By the time he finished his last portrait for the government in 1842, he had painted at least 143 and had been paid more than $3,500.[10]

King painted his first Indian portraits in the spring of 1822. His subjects were members of a large and important delegation from the Upper Missouri. The Pawnee, Oto, Omaha, Kansa, and Missouri delegates were in Washington as part of an elaborate scheme designed to influence the Upper Missouri tribes to accept peaceably American expansion into their country. These Indians were the first in King's remarkable and unique series of Indian portraits, but their experiences were typical of countless groups that visited the nation's capital in the early years of the Republic.

Portraits, Presents, and Peace Medals

The practice of inviting Indian leaders to tour America's largest cities was a major component of federal Indian policy until well into the nineteenth century. Too weak to risk war with the powerful tribes arrayed along its borders, the federal government had to rely instead on diplomacy, intimidation, even bribery to keep the Indians friendly and peaceful. Bringing a tribe's most important leaders to eastern cities, especially Washington, allowed the fullest use of all these expedients. After meeting the president, being showered with presents and attention, and then inspecting carefully selected military installations, few of the unsophisticated natives returned to their people without profound respect for American power and wealth.

Taking care of the Indian visitors was no easy task, for scarcely a week went by in the 1820s without the arrival in the capital of another delegation. Not all came for the same reasons, of course. Some came to air tribal grievances, others to negotiate treaties, and a few for no real purpose other than to do a little sightseeing. Since the government had to pay all the expenses for these junkets, trips in the latter category were ruled out unless the Indians agreed to pay for them out of their annuity allowances. As McKenney explained to one inquirer, "the rule of the [War] Department in regard to paying the expenses of Agents and Indians visiting the Seat of Government is this—when the object of the visit is one in which the government is interested; and when a visit is deemed essential to a better understanding of that object, and which could not be so well had by correspondence—and when permission to make the visit is given, by the Department."[11]

The invitation to visit Washington was normally prompted by a request from an Indian agent. "The Chiefs and principal men of the most numerous nations of Indians within my agency, who have had but little intercourse with the Americans, have frequently expressed a great disposition to be permitted to visit the great American Chief, and to see the wealth and strength of our nation, about which they have heard so much, when they are still unwilling to believe, that it does far exceed their own," wrote the Upper Missouri agent Benjamin O'Fallon to the secretary of war in April 1821. "Therefore, I am induced to suggest . . . the importance of about fifteen of the principal Chiefs and leading men of some of the largest nations of the Missouri, and high up the Mississippi, being indulged in visiting the Seat of Government, and some of our largest Cities, [for] the purpose of forming some idea of the population of the Nation, and the wealth of our Cities. . . . Our troops have produced much respect, and our Boats additional astonishment, but many are still disposed to underrate our strength, to believe that the detachment of Troops on the Missouri, is not a part, but the whole of our army."[12] If the secretary of war agreed that the purpose for the visit was a good one—as in this case—the Indians would be allowed to come.

Pennsylvania Avenue in Washington, D.C., as it appeared in 1830. National Archives.

Anticipating a lively winter in the East after two years at his wilderness outpost, O'Fallon, a handsome bachelor, acted quickly. He sent runners to the tribes near Council Bluffs, inviting the chiefs and warriors to visit their Great Father in Washington; in less than a month he was traveling east, accompanied by his black body servant, two interpreters, and seventeen Kansa, Missouri, Omaha, Oto, and Pawnee Indians.

The proud, warlike Pawnees, led by Sharitarish, brother of head chief Tarecawawaho, dominated the delegation. Confident in the belief that the president of the United States could not have as many wives and warriors as he had, Tarecawawaho refused to humble himself by visting the Great Father; but he had no objection to sending thirty-year-old Sharitarish as his representative. Accompanying him were Peskelechaco, of the Republican Pawnees, and Petalesharro, chief of the Pawnee Loups. Tall, handsome, only twenty-four, his bravery attested to by his full war bonnet of eagle feathers, Petalesharro four years earlier had saved a captive Comanche woman from being burned at the stake. Opposed to human sacrifice, he had rushed from the crowd, cut the woman free, thrown her across a horse, and carried her from the Pawnee village.

Less militant, though no less colorful, were the other delegates. Leading the Omaha deputation was Ongpatonga, or Big Elk, their principal chief. This distinguished orator was about forty and was considered the most talented and influential member of his tribe. Ably representing the Otos were Choncape, or Big Kansas, and Shaumonekusse, or Prairie Wolf, who was accompanied by his young wife, Hayne Hudjihini, or Eagle of Delight. The principal Kansa delegate was Monchousia, or White Plume.

Supervising this diverse and temperamental group challenged O'Fallon's abilities. The Missouris, Omahas, and Otos were peaceful and amicable, "deserving the friendship and confidence of the American people," but the agent considered the Kansas "impudent" and the Pawnees "insolent."[13] The troublesome Kansas were at war with most of their neighbors, creating additional tensions within the delegation. Communication was also a major problem. The delegates represented two language groups, and none of them spoke English. Consequently, interpreters had to translate all instructions and messages twice.

No matter; O'Fallon considered himself capable of coping with any situation. Although only twenty-six, he had already seen many years' service as a fur trader and Indian agent, working for his uncle, William Clark, the superintendent of Indian affairs at St. Louis, who had raised him from infancy. Because of his long association with Clark, O'Fallon was remarkably well schooled in the customs, habits, and character of the Indians of the Upper Missouri. Arrogant, quick-tempered, and fast with his fists, he scorned agents who handled their Indians in a "tame and humbled maner [sic]," believing they disgraced both "themselves and [the] government in the eye of the Savage." In his opinion, an Indian agent had to be a man "of the most daring, persevering, and enterprising caracter [sic]."[14]

The delegation's immediate destination was St. Louis. With the Indians quartered under his uncle's care at the superintendency, O'Fallon prepared for the rigorous 900 miles ahead. He reshod the horses and mules, and purchased draft horses, a harness, two dearborn wagons, and such incidentals as nine pounds of tobacco, three pounds of vermilion, and six pairs of stirrups. He also added two men to the company: James Graves, a black, hired as cook for the Indians until they reached Washington; and Louis T. Honore, his uncle's interpreter and secretary, whom Clark may have sent along to keep a protective eye on his hard-drinking, hot-tempered young nephew. In any event, Honore served O'Fallon well, handling all business matters and attending to the delegates. While O'Fallon kept busy elsewhere, the Indians evidently amused themselves by eating, for they consumed some four hundred and fifty pounds of beef in twelve days.

On the morning of October 19 the colorful cavalcade resumed its trek. Riding in the lead was the confident O'Fallon, reins in one hand, his ever present cigar in the other. Strung out behind him in full regalia were the somber, apprehensive Indians. Lumbering along in the rear were the wagons, driven by the two blacks and piled high with provisions, bedding, and gifts for the president.

Sleeping at inns where possible, or camping along the road, the Indians traveled for six weeks by way of Louisville, Wheeling, and Hagerstown. On November 30 the *National Intelligencer* announced the delegation's triumphant arrival in Washington. "Their object is to visit their Great Father, and learn something of that civilization of which they have hitherto remained in total ignorance," the paper reported. Representing the "most

remote tribes with which we have intercourse," the delegates were thought to be "the first of those tribes that have ever been in the midst of our settlements."

Surprisingly, O'Fallon did not board with his charges in the capital. Perhaps he had seen enough of them during the preceding three months. The first four days he and his body servant stayed at the Indian Queen, Washington's most popular hotel, advertising sixty "well-proportioned and well-furnished" rooms; then he moved to an equally fine inn owned by Joshua Tennison on Pennsylvania Avenue. The Indians and interpreters, however, he lodged a block away at George Miller's tavern, a notorious establishment where slave dealers reputedly housed their property while traveling through Washington. Apparently, Miller's price was right. He charged O'Fallon only seventy-five cents a day for each delegate's room and board, half the amount the agent paid at the Indian Queen and Tennison's inn.

Service at the Indian Queen was typical of that of hotels in this period. Jesse Brown, the proprietor, would welcome new arrivals at the curbstone as they alighted from their stages and then usher them into the inn under the large swinging sign with its brightly painted portrait of Pocahontas. A servant would carry the luggage to the rooms. At meal times Brown met the guests at the dining room door, carved the main dishes, and helped with the serving. Decanters of whiskey and brandy were furnished at no extra charge. Room service was provided by bell cords connected to rows of bells hanging behind the bar. The bartender also had to act as desk clerk, seeing that the bells were answered, receiving and delivering messages, and giving information. The cost to the Indian office for each member of a delegation at this hotel was $1.25 a day, a price that included meals and room, but not laundry, barbering, and the like.[15]

For the next few days the bewildered visitors were set upon by tailors, cobblers, and merchants who measured them for hats, shirts, trousers, and boots. The men received military uniforms—blue greatcoats with red cuffs and capes and silver epaulettes, blue trousers, and black leather boots. The hats resembled a coronet decorated with red and blue foil and brightly colored feathers. Silver armbands, tomahawks, sheath knives, and powder horns completed the ensembles. Eagle of Delight was given scarlet pantaloons and a

Indian Queen Hotel
Washington City

Maj. O'Fallon
                    To Jesse Brown Dr.
1821

Nov. 28th To 6 Suppers & Lodgings — 4..50
      " Whisky ——————— "..75
29 " Whisky ——————— "..124
30 " Segars 124 ditto 124 — "..25
Dec. 1 " Beer 124 (2) Toddy 1..25 1..374
2 " Breakfasts & Dinners for } 4..25
   " 4 Indians & Interpreter }
   " Board for Self 4 Days — 4..00
   " Fire in Chambers ——— 2..50
                          $21..75

Recd Payment

Geo. B Blackwell
for
Jesse Brown

Opposite: Top, Jesse Brown's Indian Queen Hotel, Washington's most popular inn of that day. Library of Congress. ▪ Bottom, bill from the Indian Queen for members of the Indian delegation supervised by agent O'Fallon. National Archives.

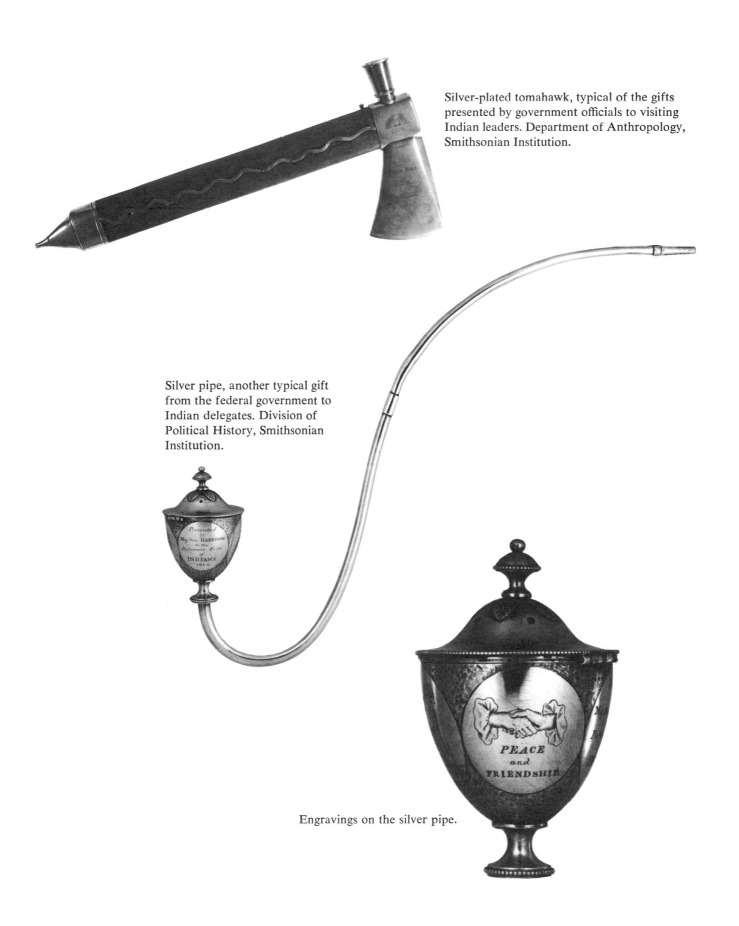

Silver-plated tomahawk, typical of the gifts presented by government officials to visiting Indian leaders. Department of Anthropology, Smithsonian Institution.

Silver pipe, another typical gift from the federal government to Indian delegates. Division of Political History, Smithsonian Institution.

Engravings on the silver pipe.

green cambric cloak. The Indians were evidently pleased with the clothes because Shaumone-kusse more than twenty years later was still proudly wearing his greatcoat, which, an observer noted, was "adorned with red facings and enormously large brass buttons, and garnished upon each shoulder with a pair of tarnished, sickly-looking silver epaulettes." The rest of the costume had evidently long since been discarded, however, because "from beneath the skirts of the coat appeared two bare legs; and . . . a pair of coarse moccasins of buffalo hide."[16]

By far the most important gifts given the Indians were peace medals and American flags. They carried the full weight of national allegiance and conferred upon the recipients added status and rank within their tribes. French and Spanish explorers began the practice of giving medals to the Indians, and the British and Americans continued the custom. Bearing the likeness of the incumbent president, the solid-silver American medals were made in three sizes. The largest medals, about three inches in diameter, were presented to the most important chiefs; smaller medals went to chiefs and warriors of correspondingly lesser rank. The different sizes were very important because they recognized hierarchies of leadership within a tribe.[17]

The Indians regarded a medal as a prized possession, to be buried with the owner when he died or to be handed down from generation to generation. Possession of a medal was such an important status symbol that leading warriors were very much offended if they did not receive one. During the audience with President James Monroe, for example, Eagle of Delight noted that medals had not been distributed to all members of the delegation. She said that the "Great Father had given the red men new clothes like white men, and they looked very well in them," but "those who had no silver medals would look still better if they had them."[18]

The flags presented with the medals were purchased by McKenney from Philadelphia merchants who made them in two sizes according to the superintendent's specifications. Their stripes resembled those on the official American flag, but the fields carried as a device an eagle, stars, or both as in the case of the larger flags. The device was handpainted on both sides of the fabric—rough bunting which, McKenney noted, looked crude but was long lasting. The large flags measured seven feet six inches by four feet eight inches and cost twelve dollars, including tassels and cord.

The delegations usually remained three or four weeks in Washington, with several more weeks spent visiting New York, Philadelphia, and Baltimore. If the main order of business was the negotiation of a treaty, however, a delegation might stay in the

This is one of the flags presented to prominent chiefs by the government. Chicago Historical Society.

capital as long as six months. The Indians would visit theaters, circuses, churches, museums, and farms; inspect battleships, navy yards, and forts; and meet with church groups and civic organizations.

During its stay in Washington the highlight for every delegation was an audience with the Great Father, the president of the United States. In a White House ceremony which included the pomp and pageantry accorded visiting heads of state, speeches and gifts were exchanged and the president then placed peace medals around the necks of the Indians. The lighting and passing around of peace pipes would generally end the ceremony; then wine, cake, and other refreshments would be served to the participants.

Members of the O'Fallon delegation were wearing their new finery when the Indians formally met President Monroe at the White House on February 4, 1822. Followed by O'Fallon and the interpreters, they were ushered into the president's antechamber where they nervously awaited his arrival. They were not completely at ease in their strange clothes. "Their coats seemed to pinch them about the shoulders," one bystander noticed; "now and then they would take off their uneasy headdresses, and one sought a temporary relief by pulling off his boots."[19] Monroe's entrance brought the assembly to attention.

Speaking from prepared notes held in one hand, the president addressed the delegates, thanking them for coming such a great distance to see him and the wonders of the white man's world. Now, he hoped the Indians would want the comforts of civilized life for themselves. If so, he was prepared to send missionaries to teach their people agriculture and Christianity. The president was also pleased that the Indians had visited forts, arsenals, and navy yards, but, he warned, they had seen only a fraction of American strength. Few fighting men were needed at the capital; in time of war all citizens took up arms and became warriors. Thus, he urged the Indians to remain at peace with each other and not to listen to those who advised them to mistrust or fight with the United States. As Monroe spoke, the interpreters translated his speech sentence by sentence; the Indians in turn nodded gravely, indicating that they understood what had been said.

When the president finished, the delegates were invited to respond. Sharitarish stepped forward, solemnly shook hands with Monroe, and slowly delivered a long speech. "My Great Father," he said, "I have traveled a great distance to see you—I have seen you and my heart rejoices. I have heard your words . . . and I will carry them to my people as pure as they came from your mouth. . . . [I] have seen your people, your homes, your vessels on the big lake, and a great many wonderful things far beyond my comprehension, which appears to have been made by the Great Spirit and placed in your hands." But, wonderful as it was, he would not trade his way of life for that of the white man. There were still plenty of buffalo to hunt and beaver to trap. "It is too soon," Sharitarish continued, "to send those good men [the missionaries] among us—we are not starving yet—we wish you to permit us to enjoy the chase until the game of our country is exhausted—until the wild animals become extinct. . . . I have grown up, and lived this long without work," he declared; "I am in hopes you will suffer me to die without it. We have everything we want— we have plenty of land, if you will keep your people off it."[20]

The other chiefs then spoke in turn, each stressing his love for the Indian way of life. The first speakers were noticeably nervous, but each succeeding orator became less reserved until the last—claimed a witness—spoke "as loud as you ever heard a lawyer at a county court bar."[21]

As each speaker finished, he laid a present at the president's feet. By the end of the ceremony, Monroe was sitting behind a mound of buffalo robes, calumets, moccasins, and feathered headdresses. Sharitarish explained that the Indians knew the gifts would be of little value to him, but they wanted Monroe "to have them deposited and preserved in some conspicuous part of your lodge, so that when we are gone . . . if our children should visit this place, as we do now, they may see and recognize with pleasure the deposits of their fathers, and reflect on the times that are past."[22] What became of the gifts is unknown; only the chiefs' portraits remain.

By the end of the lengthy ceremony, the audience had been swelled considerably by curious onlookers, including several Supreme Court justices who were waiting to see the president. Everyone adjourned to the drawing room for cake and wine. The Indians capped the festivities by lighting their pipes and passing them to President Monroe, Chief Justice John Marshall, and other dignitaries, who took token whiffs. By this time the visitors had endured long enough their unfamiliar and uncomfortable clothing. As a dismayed observer reported, "one of them, unable longer to bear the pressure of his boots, sat down and deliberately pulled them off. Another his coat, until the whole might have brought themselves back to a comfortable state of nature had they not been led out."[23]

The Indians met the president on two other occasions. A month earlier, New Year's Day, 1822, they had been part of the crush at the annual White House reception. While the Marine Band played a medley of patriotic airs, cabinet officials, members of the diplomatic corps and Congress, and military officers chatted amiably with each other as they elbowed their way to the punch bowls. Shortly before the afternoon reception was to end, the Indians stalked into the East Room—and stole the show from the fashionably dressed ladies of Washington. The Indians were arrayed in their finest ceremonial garb; three were wrapped in brightly painted buffalo robes, including Petalesharro, who was also wearing his war bonnet with feathers "descending like wings to the waist." Bright vermilion made their faces even more awesome. To Jonathan Elliot, editor of the *Washington Gazette,* they looked "cadaverous" until the "music and hilarity of the scene" put them at ease; then "in place of pensive gravity, a heartfelt joy beamed in the sullen eye of the Indian warrior."[24]

Their last meeting with President Monroe was on Saturday, February 9, when they danced for him on the enclosure just north of the White House. Well publicized by the local press and favored with a crisp, sunny day, the spectacle attracted half the population of Washington, including many ladies and most of the congressmen, who had adjourned early for the occasion. The mock council between the Indians and the presidential party, which opened the show, afforded "a striking specimen of native oratory," in one bystander's opinion. "The gestures of the Indian speakers were violent, but energetic, and frequently graceful." When the conference ended, the warriors threw aside their blankets and, armed with tomahawks and clubs, performed dances described as "a rude kind of leaping, governed, in some measure, by the sullen sound of a sort of drum." Wearing nothing but war paint and red flannel breechclouts, the Indians "uttered shocking yells, and writhed and twisted their bodies in frightful contortion." The three-hour theatrical was a tremendous success. "They were painted horribly, and exhibited the operation of scalping and tomahawking in fine style," a second observer claimed. Still another thought the exhibition one which "no person of liberal and philosophical curiosity would willingly have missed seeing, and which no one who viewed it . . . would choose to witness again."[25]

The Indians so impressed Washingtonians with their dignified and orderly behavior that, in addition to making the usual round of balls and parties, many of the delegates were invited to private homes for tea or to spend an evening by the fireside. Shaumone-kusse and his wife were frequent guests of Jonathan Barber, a local physician. "She was a very good natured, mild woman," Barber wrote, whereas her husband "shewed great readiness in acquiring our language, retaining anything that he was once informed, and imitating the tones of every word." The Indians also demonstrated a natural wit. On one occasion the doctor showed several of them a skeleton he kept in a closet, whereupon one of them grasped a bony hand and said, "How you do?"[26]

The most popular delegate was Petalesharro, whose dramatic rescue of the captive woman fired the imaginations of romantic easterners. The girls of Miss White's Seminary immortalized the deed by having an elaborate silver medal engraved for him. The front shows Petalesharro and the woman rushing toward two horses; the reverse shows several disappointed warriors looking at the empty scaffold. The inscription reads: "TO THE

Choncape and Sharitarish, by John Neagle, 1821. Historical Society of Pennsylvania.

BRAVEST OF THE BRAVE." The girls presented the medal at a private home in a ceremony witnessed by the entire delegation. Touched by the gesture, Petalesharro clutched the medal and said: "I am glad that my brothers and sisters have heard of the good act that I have done. My brothers and sisters think that I did it in ignorance, but I now know what I have done."[27]

Eagle of Delight also enjoyed a large share of the limelight. "The *squa* excited great attention," wrote Laura Wirt, daughter of the attorney general, after meeting her at the home of the French ambassador. "She was dressed in a scarlet stuff robe, trimmed very fine with gold lace; and presented by the President. She . . . is quite a pretty woman. At least, she is, no doubt considered so in her own nation, and even with us, her modest, goodnatured countenance would pass here for comely, notwithstanding her broad face and high cheek bones. She is not more than fifteen they say, tho' I should think her two or three years older. She is the favorite wife of one of the Chiefs, and for that reason accompanied him." The French ambassador had promised to lead off the first cotillion with "Madame Le Squa," but he could not coax the reluctant debutante into dancing. Needless to say, Laura Wirt confided to a friend, "there has been nothing else talked of since these Indians have been here, and a vast many more anecdotes are related of them than I shall undertake to tell you."[28]

Little wonder, then, that McKenney began his portrait gallery with members of this delegation. King, however, missed the honor of being the first white artist to capture them on canvas because, a week after arriving in Washington, most of the Indians continued on to Baltimore, Philadelphia, and New York, returning to the capital two days after Christmas. While in Philadelphia, Sharitarish, Choncape, and Petalesharro posed for

Petalesharro [Generous Chief], Pawnee, by Charles Bird King. Gulf States Paper Corporation.

Opposite: Top, Young Omawhaw, War Eagle, Little Missouri, and Pawnees, by Charles Bird King. National Collection of Fine Arts, Smithsonian Institution. ■ Left, Hayne Hudjihini, or Eagle of Delight, Oto, by Charles Bird King. Danish National Museum.■ Right, Eagle of Delight. White House Collection. ■ **Below:** Eagle of Delight. Gulf States Paper Corporation.

Shaumonekusse [Prairie Wolf], Oto, by Charles Bird King. Gulf States Paper Corporation.

Choncape [Big Kansas], Oto, by Charles Bird King. Danish National Museum.

Ongpatonga [Big Elk], Omaha, by Charles Bird King. Thomas Gilcrease Institute of American History and Art.

Monchousia [White Plume], Kansa, by Charles Bird King. Danish National Museum.

the celebrated John Neagle. These portraits today are in the Historical Society of Pennsylvania.

King's portraits, however, especially those of Petalesharro and Eagle of Delight, were the ones that captured the popular imagination. Exactly how many portraits from this delegation he executed remains a mystery. Certainly it was a considerable number. McKenney selected eight of the seventeen delegates for his archives: the Pawnee chiefs Sharitarish, Peskelechaco, and Petalesharro; the Otos Choncape, Shaumonekusse, and Eagle of Delight; the Omaha orator Ongpatonga; and the Kansa chief Monchousia. King, in addition, did a portrait of each member of the delegation, which the Indians took home with them. For these twenty-five paintings, King received $300 from the War Department. King also did copies of the eight primary subjects for himself, and it is these copies that spawned the many replicas of Petalesharro, Eagle of Delight, and Shaumonekusse that are extant today. According to William Faux, a British traveler in Washington at the time, the Indians "excited so much interest from their dignified personal appearance, and from their peaceful manner, that they received a great number of rich presents . . . [including their portraits], which are gone with them. [These] were taken in oil by Mr. King in their native costume, buffalo skins, with the hair inside, turned back at the neck and breast, which looked very handsome, like fur collars. Eight, however, the chiefs and the squaw, Mr. King copied and keeps himself." The portraits were obviously well publicized because Laura Wirt also commented on them. "I must try to see their likenesses which Mr. King has been taking, to their infinite amusement and delight," she informed her friend.[29]

King painted at least one other oil portrait of this delegation. Entitled simply *Young Omahaw, War Eagle, Little Missouri, and Pawnees,* it is a group portrait of five members of the delegation. The canvas was not part of McKenney's gallery and seems to have been a studio study King may have painted after the Indians left Washington. In any case, the magnificent study is considered one of King's finest efforts, a marvelous combination of technical skill, color, and creativity. This original oil was presented to the Smithsonian Institution in 1946 by Mrs. Helen Barlow of London.

One other portrait from this delegation deserves mention, that of Petalesharro by Samuel F. B. Morse. This artist, better known for his inventive genius, included Petalesharro's portrait in his monumental *The Old House of Representatives,* which he painted in Washington in 1822. Since Morse hoped to stabilize his shaky financial resources by taking this painting on tour and charging admission, he obviously tried to capitalize on Petalesharro's popularity by placing him in the House gallery, watching the preparations for an evening session. Interestingly, the solitary Indian, identified only as "Pawnee Chief" in Morse's key to the painting, closely resembles the portrait of Petalesharro by Charles Bird King.

The delegation remained in Washington until the end of February; the King portraits evidently were the last order of business. For the return trip, the party used commercial transportation; O'Fallon had auctioned away the horses and wagons shortly after the Indians returned from their eastern tour. From Washington, the delegates traveled by

stagecoach to Wheeling, where the agent bought a flatboat that carried them to Louisville. There they booked steamboat passage to St. Louis, arriving April 5. O'Fallon reported that they were "all in fine health and spirits, and most favorably impressed with the strength, wealth, and magnanimity of our Nation"—an impression enforced by the 1,700 pounds of presents they brought home.[30]

When the Indians reached their respective villages, they found that they had long since been given up for dead, and their unexpected arrival touched off widespread rejoicing. O'Fallon, however, had little cause for celebrating. The agent had lost a horse and his "most faithful and valuable servant," who had drowned while swimming across the swollen west fork of the Grand River. Furthermore, he claimed to be suffering "worse from fatigue and exposure than I had ever experienced before."[31]

Although the delegation's visit cost the federal government $6,085, it was considered money well spent, as this editorial from the *Washington Gazette* indicates: "The object of their interesting mission, we believe, has been fully accomplished: these aborigines are deeply impressed with the power of the long-knives, that for the future the tomahawk will not be raised with their consent, against their white brethren."[32] And the tribes from which the delegates came did remain remarkably peaceful as the inexorable tide of white settlement reached the headwaters of the Missouri.

What became of the delegates? Eagle of Delight died of measles within weeks of her return from Washington. The grief-stricken Shaumonekusse vowed to fast to death, but friends forced him to eat, and he lived to become head chief of the Otos. In 1823, upon the death of his brother, Sharitarish became chief of the Grand Pawnees, only to die himself within a year. The Pawnee chief Peskelechaco died in 1826, killed while leading a counterattack against an Osage war party that had raided his village. Petalesharro lived until 1841, becoming one of the most respected and influential leaders of the Pawnees.

As for McKenney, he lost his job as superintendent of Indian trade just three months after the O'Fallon delegation left Washington. Congress abolished the Office of Indian Trade in May 1822, claiming the trading houses were wasteful and inefficient. It was only a temporary setback for the resilient McKenney. In less than two years he was once again at the helm of the nation's Indian interests, this time as head of the newly formed Bureau of Indian Affairs, and one of his first acts was to reestablish his Archives of the American Indian.

More Delegations–More Portraits

The Bureau of Indian Affairs opened for business on March 16, 1824. It was created especially for McKenney by Secretary of War John C. Calhoun, who owed the colonel a political debt. During the two years McKenney had been out of office, he had established and edited the *Washington Republican and Congressional Examiner,* a newspaper dedicated to promoting Calhoun's candidacy for the 1824 presidential nomination. Calhoun eventually withdrew from the race in return for the vice presidency, and he rewarded McKenney with the appointment to the position of superintendent of Indian affairs.

In taking the new post, McKenney accepted a responsibility of major proportions. He handled annually up to one million dollars in appropriated funds; and he supervised the activities of twenty Indian agents, twenty-seven subagents, three territorial governors who served ex officio as superintendents of Indian affairs, another superintendent at St. Louis, plus additional personnel who brought the total number to nearly one hundred persons. To help him with the administrative workload, McKenney had two clerks and a messenger, who shared his small office on the second floor of the War Department building.

Even in his new position McKenney found time for his Archives of the American Indian. What disposition had been made of the archives during his absence from public office is unknown. Although some of the curiosities were sold at public auction during the liquidation of the factory system, it is unlikely that McKenney would have allowed the sale of anything but duplicates. He did, in fact, preserve part of his collection by presenting "thirty specimens Indian Dresses and Ornaments" to the Columbian Institute of Washington. The remainder, including the portraits of the O'Fallon delegation, McKenney probably transferred to the War Department building, because shortly after assuming his new duties he referred to the "Indian curiosities which are deposited here."[33]

Although he no longer had the ready access to public funds he had enjoyed in his former position, McKenney continued to collect. Some items were received in response to formal requests for donations. For example, on May 22, 1824, he appealed to all the superintendents of schools in the Indian country for "Any specimens of birds, minerals, Indian costumes or other curiosities, which you can conveniently & without expense command & forward, also seeds of indigenous plants with their names & virtues, will be very acceptable." Other artifacts, such as a string of wampum donated by a New York clergyman, were contributed by individuals who had heard about the collection.[34]

Indian delegations visiting Washington were still another productive source of objects for the archives. Since McKenney was responsible for the Indians during their stay in the capital, few left without a stop at the Indian office to view his collection. The visit invariably impressed them and it was not uncommon for the Indians to add to the

Left, John C. Calhoun, by Charles Bird King. Corcoran Gallery of Art. ■ Below, floor plan of the War Department building. McKenney's office was room 3. ■ Bottom, War Department building, 1820s.

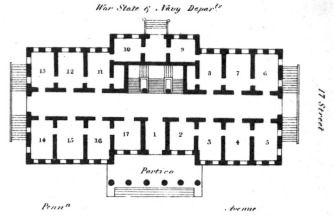

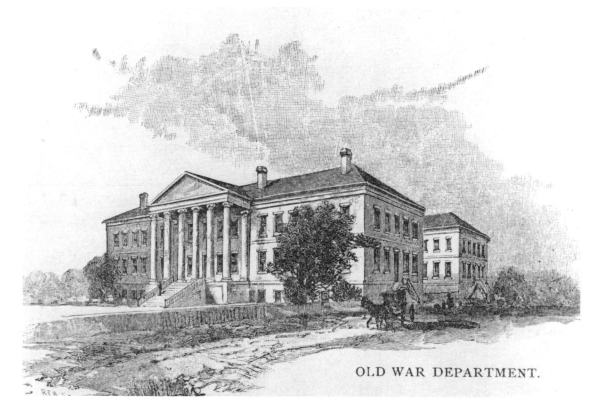

OLD WAR DEPARTMENT.

Peace medal given to Red Jacket by George Washington. Buffalo and Erie County Historical Society.

GEORGE WASHINGTON
PRESIDENT.
1792

assemblage from their own apparel. Unique items an Indian owner failed to offer, McKenney would attempt to purchase. He made an unsuccessful bid to buy Red Jacket's peace medal, tomahawk, and coat, probably hoping to complement the Seneca chief's portrait that hung in the gallery. On another occasion, the superintendent obtained two bark canoes by giving four stranded Passamaquoddy Indians $191 in food, clothing, and cash for traveling expenses.

McKenney also made contributions of his own. During his term as Indian commissioner he went on two treaty-making trips into Michigan Territory. The first trip, in the summer of 1826, was to Fond du Lac at the western tip of Lake Superior; the second, made the following summer, was to Butte des Morts in present-day Wisconsin. On the latter trip, after completing his business in the North, McKenney traveled down the Mississippi River to Memphis and then on overland through the South, visting the Chickasaw, Choctaw, and Creek Indians before returning to Washington. On these excursions he acquired many "Indian Dresses, Costumes, Minerals &c," including a complete Chippewa outfit and a British peace medal and flag.[35]

Animal skin cape and ceremonial pipe from McKenney's Indian Office museum. The cape, now in the custody of the Smithsonian Institution, belonged to Okeemakeequid, a Chippewa chief whose portrait was painted by James Otto Lewis at Fond du Lac in 1826. McKenney later reproduced the portrait in his *History of the Indian Tribes of North America*. The pipe bears an almost illegible label in McKenney's hand: "Presented in August 1824 to President James Monroe by Mahaskah, an Ioway Head Chief. T.L.McK." Department of Anthropology, Smithsonian Institution.

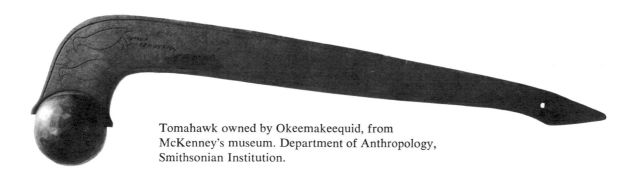

Tomahawk owned by Okeemakeequid, from McKenney's museum. Department of Anthropology, Smithsonian Institution.

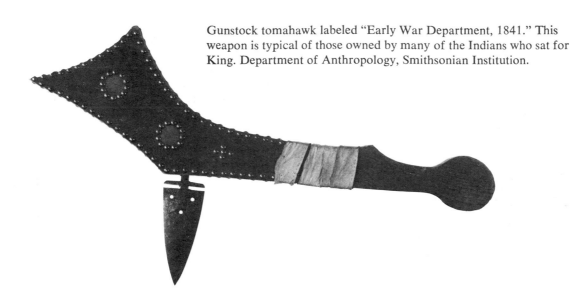

Gunstock tomahawk labeled "Early War Department, 1841." This weapon is typical of those owned by many of the Indians who sat for King. Department of Anthropology, Smithsonian Institution.

Manuscripts and books relating to the American Indian also formed a significant part of McKenney's archives. These, he once explained, he had acquired primarily for his own information and because he thought they would be useful in his work. Although he had been gathering such materials from the time he first began collecting, the complex responsibilities of the position of superintendent of Indian affairs made their acquisition more urgent, particularly since he had found the War Department "barren of anything of the kind."[36]

In his efforts to obtain such data, McKenney even turned to missionaries working among the Indians. "With the view of preserving in the archives of the Government whatever of the aboriginal man [that] can be rescued from the ultimate destruction which awaits his race," he wrote in August 1824, "I have to beg the favor of you to prepare and forward to the Department, as soon as you conveniently can, an Alphabet and Grammar, and as far as you are able, a chapter on some subject, in the language of the Tribe, or Tribes among whom you and your associates are located." And, he added, "whatever may strike you as worthy of preservation, in this, or any similar way, I will thank you to possess me of."[37] The appeal was effective. Although no doubt difficult and time-consuming to prepare, grammars evidently were compiled for the Sac, Cherokee, Shawnee, Osage, Choctaw, and Nottaway Indians. The quality varied, of course. Some were no more than mere word lists. On the other hand, the Choctaw grammar sent to him by the Reverend Alfred Wright was so well done that McKenney gave him fifty dollars.

The most impressive linguistic item in the archives was the eighty-six character Cherokee syllabary developed by George Guess, or Sequoyah, who wanted his people to have a written language. When Sequoyah visited Washington in 1828, McKenney escorted him to King's studio to ensure that his portrait would be preserved for posterity.

McKenney obtained the published works in the archives primarily from book dealers. For instance, on April 25, 1825, he instructed the firm of Davis & Force to contact its agents in Baltimore, Philadelphia, New York, and Boston "for lists of the titles and numbers of Volumes, and prices of such works, as relate to the Aborigines of the Country as are deemed to be standard Histories—Memoirs—Travels &c—Such as Heckewelders, Hunters, Longs, Schoolcrafts,—&c &c.—and any Theories of the Origin &c of the Indians; also such works as relate to the Geology of the Western Country &c. &c." The lists were to include a synopsis of each book. From them he would make his selection. Those selected were to be bound and "bound well" and then imprinted on one cover with the words "Office of Indian Affairs" and with "War Department" on the other.[38] He reversed this procedure

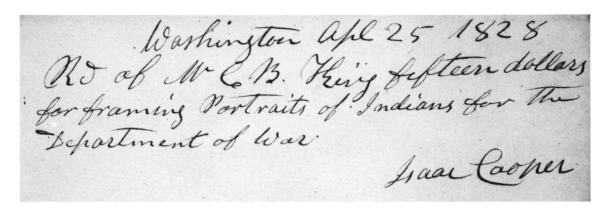

when, two years later, he provided the Baltimore publishing house of Fielding Lucas and Company with his own list of books that he wanted the firm to find. By 1828 the archives contained at least fifty-two titles purchased at a cost of more than three hundred dollars.

The expenditures for artifacts and books were trifling compared to the sums spent on the gallery of Indian portraits that McKenney regarded as the heart of his archives. Seated in his office, surrounded by the portraits, the colonel never tired of recounting at length tales of the Indians he had met on his western trips or in Washington. His enthusiasm did not escape the notice of his visitors. Nicholas Biddle, in describing a meeting he once had with McKenney, wrote: "I remember when I first saw him, he was surrounded by uncouth portraits of savages of both sexes, whose merits he explained with as much unction as a roman Cicerone—how nearly extremes touch when so civilized a gentleman was in contact with so wild & aboriginal a set."[39]

McKenney cherished his archives with the zeal of a modern curator and took pains to see that it was properly preserved, displayed, and publicized. King often framed and labeled his paintings before sending them to the Indian office. Others were framed and labeled by Isaac Cooper, who also boxed and shipped the copies of the paintings sent to the Indians. Two carpenters, on record only as Gaither and Wilson, hung the portraits and performed odd jobs around the office. In the spring of 1828 John Simpson installed two display cases, including one of glass that he made himself. Later the same year he worked three months "arranging and preserving from moth[s] &c. Indian relicks; and the paintings of Indian likenesses from injury &c."[40]

When McKenney had returned to office in 1824 he had quickly put King back to work. From St. Louis that summer, Superintendent William Clark brought seventeen Sac and Fox, Iowa, and Piankeshaw Indians to Washington. The Sac and Fox, led by Keokuk, Wakechai, and Peahmuska, and the Iowas, led by Mahaskah and Moanahonga, came to negotiate a major land cession to the United States; the two tribes, in separate treaties, surrendered their claims to northern Missouri.

The only woman accompanying the delegation was Rantchewaime, one of Mahaskah's seven wives. Although not invited, she had been determined to visit Washington and had secretly followed the Iowa delegates, making her appearance when they had gone too far to send her back. The pretty Iowa woman may have regretted her impetuousness, however, because Mahaskah would beat her after imbibing too freely of the table liquor at Tennison's hotel. On one such occasion, the Indian agent heard the commotion in Mahaskah's room and burst in on the quarreling couple. The Iowa chief, forgetting he was on the second

Note from King to McKenney, August 23, 1824: "Mr Kings Respects to Thomas M Mackeney Esq. and begs the loan of the sixteen Indians he painted for the War Office to copy for the Indian department." National Archives.

floor, tried to avoid a confrontation with the agent by escaping through a window. He lifted the sash, stepped out, and fell to the ground, breaking an arm. A few days later Mahaskah had to pose for his portrait and the painful injury is reflected in the chief's furrowed brows.[41]

The large number of portraits King executed of this delegation testifies to its importance. Not only did he paint portraits of all the delegates for the archives, for which he received $320, but he also painted copies for the Indians, which were shipped to them a few weeks after they had left Washington. King, who had to borrow the originals in order to make the copies, charged McKenney $193.50, a price that included the Indians' sixteen copies, the labels and packing cases, plus a copy of Rantchewaime's portrait for the archives. McKenney had not commissioned her portrait; the artist had done it on his own, probably anticipating a large number of orders for replicas, as had been the case with Eagle of Delight's portrait. He got at least one order—from McKenney. When the colonel saw it, he immediately ordered a copy.

The fact that the delegates were given copies of their portraits is also an indication of the government's desire to please them. Certainly this was the case with the Creek delegation from Fort Mitchell, Alabama, which visited Washington in November 1825. Led by Opothle Yoholo, the delegation hoped that the government would overthrow the dishonorable treaty of Indian Springs ratified earlier in the year. Two citizens of Georgia, serving as commissioners for the United States, had allegedly negotiated this treaty with the entire Creek Nation, but the signatory chiefs actually represented only a small portion of the tribe. By the terms of the treaty the Creeks agreed to cede all their lands in Georgia and move west of the Mississippi. The Senate quickly ratified the treaty by a vote of thirty-eight to four and President John Quincy Adams just as quickly signed it into law, even though he knew the Senate had acted too hastily. By the time the delegation representing the dispossessed Creeks arrived to protest, all Washington knew the treaty was a scandal.

Garbed in a fantastic array of white man's and tribal dress, the Creeks and their interpreters arrived at the White House for an audience with the Great Father. Opothle Yoholo's appearance, like that of his eleven companions, was remarkable for its dark and settled gloom, President Adams thought. He shook hands with them all. "I am glad to see you. We should all meet in friendship."

"We are glad to be here," responded Opothle Yoholo. "Things have happened which frightened us. We hope all will be well again."

"That is my desire also," the president replied assuringly. "I also have heard things that displeased me much, but I am sure the Secretary of War will be able to arrange matters to the satisfaction of all."[42]

Adams authorized Secretary of War James Barbour to renegotiate the controversial treaty—but with the original terms: a complete cession of the Creek lands in Georgia. This, Opothle Yoholo could not accept. The tribe would consider ceding only its holdings east of the Chattahoochee, about two-thirds of the lands in question. As the weeks dragged into months, Barbour tried to pressure the delegation into accepting the government's terms, hammering so hard for a complete cession that Opothle Yoholo, torn between the needs of his people and government demands, tried to kill himself in his room at the Indian Queen Hotel. Learning of the attempted suicide, Adams directed Barbour to accept the Chattahoochee as a boundary.

While the difficult and protracted negotiations were underway, the delegates agreed to sit for their portraits, and they demanded copies to take home. McKenney, eager to placate the angry Creeks, readily agreed. As he informed one of the delegates, the copies would not be the same size as the originals—17½ by 14 inches—but "a size more convenient and portable." Nonetheless, they would be "just as true and perfect."[43] The portrait of Coosa Tustennuggee, now in the custody of the Wilmette Historical Commission, may be one of the copies. If so, it is the only portrait given to a delegate known to be extant. On wood, like most of the Indian portraits, it measures 12 by 10 inches. The portrait is by George Cooke, a Washingtonian who may have been studying under King at the time.

Opothle Yoholo was not the only Indian visitor to Washington to attempt suicide. In fact, few Indian delegations returned to their people without suffering some illness, injury, or even loss of life. The delegates, many of them quite elderly, literally risked life and limb in making the trips, being exposed to new illnesses and dangers. For instance, one of the stagecoaches carrying the Creek delegation to Washington overturned, injuring most of the passengers.

Particularly unfortunate was the 1824 Choctaw delegation from Mississippi, which came to Washington to resolve a land dispute that had defied settlement for four years. The ten-member delegation represented the finest talent the Choctaws could command, including Pushmataha, Puckshenubbee, and Mushulatubbee, the first elected chiefs of the three political districts through which the nation was democratically governed. Each of them was a proven administrator and tested warrior. Pushmataha, in fact, held a commission in the United States Army; he and his warriors had fought the British with Andrew Jackson at the Battle of New Orleans during the War of 1812.

The delegation had hardly left Mississippi when tragedy struck. The eighty-five-year-old Puckshenubbee decided to stretch his legs at a rest stop in Kentucky and fell to his death from a fog-shrouded precipice. Nevertheless, his comrades decided to continue the journey, and arrived in the capital the last week of October.

Below: Reverse of the Black Fox portrait. The inscription in King's hand reads: "Ta-go-nis-co-te-yeh Black Fox. Cherokee Chief Painted by C. B. King Washington 1828." Two uncompleted sketches make this reverse particularly unusual. duVal Radford. ■ **Opposite:** Pushmataha on his deathbed, from lithograph in McKenney's *Memoirs.*

Pushmataha, now the senior delegate, directed the negotiations. The government wanted the Choctaws to trade most of their ancestral lands in Mississippi, plus extensive holdings in Arkansas, for a large area west of Arkansas Territory that would be theirs permanently. The delegates refused to discuss Mississippi, and they would consider selling only that part of their Arkansas holdings most thickly populated with white settlers.

"Do you want us to give up farming and become hunters?" Pushmataha asked. "Take us to the western boundary of Arkansas Territory, and you will take all our valuable land."

"Good chief," replied John Calhoun, then secretary of war, "you are contradicting yourself. When we were trying to sell you those lands in 1820 you insisted they were all rocks and hills, and that the waters were only fit to overflow the crops, put out fires, and float canoes. What is the meaning of this great change?"

"I can only say, good father, that I am imitating the white man. In 1820 we wanted to buy; now we are anxious to sell."[44]

The negotiations dragged on for weeks. The government offered the Choctaws $65,000—$5,000 in cash and an annual annuity of $6,000 for ten years—if they would agree to the trade; the Choctaws demanded $450,000. The price was "wholly inadmissible," Calhoun replied. The delegates finally accepted a package deal for cash and annuities totaling $216,000. The treaty was signed in Calhoun's office on January 22, 1825, almost three months after the delegation came to Washington.

If settling this boundary dispute cost more than anticipated, so did the delegation's living expenses, which amounted to $7,463.56. Only about $2,000 was for room and board; the rest went for clothing, $1,771; liquor, $2,149.50; transportation, $960; oysters and brandy, $394.75; and such incidentals as bootblacking, $75; barbering, $58; and laundry, $25.71. McKenney was outraged by the bill, particularly the incredible sum spent for liquor. He insisted that the delegation pay half of the bar and refectory bill, or $1,469.50, leaving the government's share at $6,000, not including the considerable sum spent on Pushmataha's medical care and funeral.

The renowned warrior had died of the croup late in the negotiations. Too much liquor, the Indian agent charged; more likely, the seventy-year-old leader could not shake a persistent cold in the damp, chill Washington weather. He collapsed on the street

Pushmataha's gravestone in Congressional Cemetery, Washington, D.C.

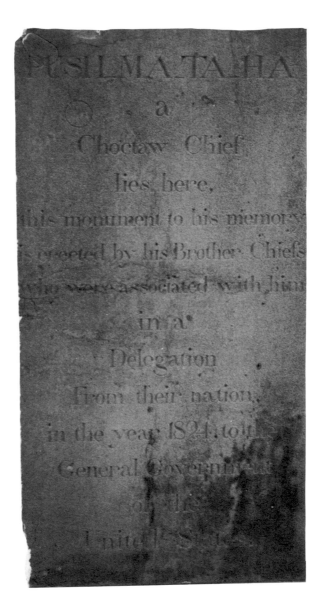

early on the morning of December 23; two physicians tended Pushmataha until he died on Christmas Eve. Certain of his approaching death, the old chief called for his weapons and trophies of war and asked that "the big guns be fired over me."[45]

Pushmataha's request for a military funeral was honored the day after Christmas by the Marine Corps under the direction of the secretary of the navy and two companies of the D. C. militia. Two thousand congressmen, government officials, and citizens followed the cortege to Congressional Cemetery beside the Anacostia River. The guns that thundered on Capitol Hill were echoed by three crisp musket volleys at the graveside as America paid tribute to a fallen warrior. Far different was this service from the meager rites given Puckshenubbee, whose Kentucky funeral cost the government only $11.87—for music, shrouding, and coffin.

McKenney may have wished for similar economy. The Indian office laid Pushmataha to rest in "Drilling Panteloons and 1 Ruffle Shirt" and in a mahogany coffin with a liner and case. McKenney rented thirteen hacks for the funeral, including one for the Reverend William Hawley, rector of St. John's Church, who also received ten dollars for his services. Altogether the medical and funeral expenses came to $147.32. They could easily have been more, but McKenney did his best to keep the costs down. On Christmas Day the attending physician sent McKenney his bill for twenty dollars for "attending to Genl Push-a-ma-ta-ha preparing and administering four injections to him while on his Death Bed—together with all other necessary attentions until he was buried."[46] McKenney, who by this point had lost the Christmas spirit, thought the charge too much and allowed the doctor only ten dollars.

The boundary dispute had been settled, but at a terrific price. The government paid roughly $8,000 for expenses; the tribe absorbed another $2,000. The cost to the Choctaws was even greater, for two of the tribe's most important leaders were dead. Fortunately, early in the deliberations, McKenney had persuaded Pushmataha to sit for his portrait. The magnificent oil is now in Tuscaloosa, Alabama, the property of the Gulf States Paper Corporation.

Not all the portraits in the gallery were commissioned personally by McKenney. Many were commissioned and sent to him by federal officials in the field. Credit for this idea belongs to Governor Lewis Cass of Michigan Territory, who in December 1824 sent McKenney a "striking likeness" of Tecumseh's brother, the Prophet, painted by James Otto Lewis, a Detroit artist of limited ability. Cass suggested that he be allowed to pay Lewis $200 from War Department funds to paint the portraits of other important Indians who visited Detroit. McKenney accepted the suggestion but asked that Lewis enlarge his small watercolor sketches to match the size of the other portraits in the Indian office. At the same time the colonel wrote to William Clark and Governor William P. Duval of Florida Territory authorizing them to spend up to a hundred dollars for portraits of "a few of your most distinguished Indian Chiefs, which should be taken in the costume of the respective Tribes who may be represented by them."[47]

The exact number of paintings McKenney acquired in this manner is uncertain. No record has been found that Governor Duval complied with the request, but McKenney did receive two portraits, which cost ten dollars each, from Clark.

The arrangement with Lewis proved far more productive. Between 1825 and 1827, the Detroit artist accompanied Governor Cass on three treaty-making trips into the Indian country and painted some two hundred and fifty Indian portraits. Of these, about forty-five were sent to McKenney, who then had them copied in oils for the archives. Athanasius Ford, a local artist, did eleven of the copies; King evidently did the others. Although Lewis received $609 for his services, he felt cheated and later tried to get additional compensation. In 1841, more than fourteen years later, Lewis petitioned Congress for more money, complaining that the government had not paid him enough initially for the thousands of miles traveled and the years spent "in the toil and labor" of obtaining the portraits. "In accomplishing that arduous task," he explained, "your petitioner expended a large portion of

Left, Jackopa, Chippewa, by Charles Bird King after James Otto Lewis. This portrait may have survived the Smithsonian fire of 1865. National Collection of Fine Arts, Smithsonian Institution. ■ Right, Esmeboin, or Cosneboin, Chippewa, by Charles Bird King after James Otto Lewis. This portrait may also have survived the Smithsonian fire. National Collection of Fine Arts, Smithsonian Institution.

his life, and undermined a Constitution, once vigorous and healthy, by encountering the rigorous vicissitudes incident to our North Western frontier." The Senate Committee on Indian affairs rejected the request.[48]

The gallery grew rapidly until the spring of 1827 when Secretary of War Barbour informed McKenney that "nearly all the likenesses have been collected which it is desirable to obtain. . . ." No more money was to be spent on portraits "unless indeed the subject be remarkable and have claims to the remembrance of posterity for some deeds of virtue or prowess; or be in figure or in costume very peculiar indeed."[49] Barbour probably was more concerned about the cost than the comprehensiveness of the gallery, for certainly the paintings were expensive. In five years McKenney had spent more than $3,100 on the gallery alone. This was a considerable sum, particularly for something not readily justified as a departmental expenditure.

Barbour's worries were well founded. Congressman Thomas P. Moore of Kentucky was appalled at the thought of spending such sums "for the pictures of these wretches the use of which it would be impossible to tell. I believe they are hung up in McKenney's room at Washington, to gratify the curiosity of strangers." When the Retrenchment Committee investigating unnecessary spending by government agencies also took exception to the gallery, McKenney felt compelled to answer the charges publicly. In a letter "To a Friend" published in local newspapers shortly after the committee's report was read in Congress, the colonel stoutly defended the expenditures for the gallery. "Apart from the great object of preserving in some form, the resemblance of an interesting people . . . it is the *policy* of the thing. Indians are like other people in many respects—and are not less sensible than we are to marks of respect and attention." All Indian delegations to Washington see the collection, he pointed out. "They see this mark of respect to their people, and respect it. Its effects, as is known to me, are, in this view of the subject, highly valuable." But, if money was all that interested Congress, the gallery could easily be sold for double its original cost. "And with it may go, without any regret of mine, *of a personal kind,* all the little relics which in my travels I have picked up, and at great trouble brought home with me. *It is no fancy scheme of mine."*[50]

McKenney did gain a measure of comfort from the final report of the Retrenchment Committee because the minority members came to his defense. Rather than censure him for this expenditure they felt that he should be provided with a larger office, "in which might be more advantageously exhibited the portraits in question, and others which may be added to them, together with an ample collection of the arms, costumes, household

Pushmataha [The Sapling Is Ready for Him], Choctaw, by Charles Bird King. Gulf States Paper Corporation.

Coosa Tustennugge

Opposite: Top left, Tagoniscoteyeh [Black Fox], Cherokee, by Charles Bird King. duVal Radford. ■ Right, Tenskwautawaw [The Prophet], Shawnee, by Charles Bird King after James Otto Lewis. Thomas Gilcrease Institute of American History and Art. ■ Bottom left, Coosa Tustennuggee, Creek, by George Cooke. Wilmette Historical Commission. ■ Right, Kitcheewabeshas [The Good Martin], Chippewa, by Charles Bird King after James Otto Lewis. Gulf States Paper Corporation. ■ **Above:** Mistippee [Benjamin], Creek, by Charles Bird King. Sotheby Parke Bernet Inc., New York.

Above: Red Jacket, Seneca, by Charles Bird King. Albright-Knox Art Gallery; gift of the Seymour H. Knox Foundation, Inc. ■ **Opposite:** Top left, Young Cornplanter, Seneca, by Charles Bird King. Danish National Museum. ■ Right, Apauly Tustennuggee, Creek, by Charles Bird King. National Collection of Fine Arts, Smithsonian Institution. ■ Bottom left, Moanahonga [Great Walker], Iowa, by Charles Bird King. Thomas Gilcrease Institute of American History and Art. ■ Right, Tulcee Mathla, Seminole, by Charles Bird King. Lowe Art Commission.

Mak-we-hai-mak, Soway Chief.
(Great Walker.)

61

Rantchewaime [Female Flying Pigeon], Iowa, by Charles Bird King. Gulf States
Paper Corporation.

Mahaskah [White Cloud], Iowa, by Charles Bird King. Thomas Gilcrease Institute of American History and Art.

David Vann, Cherokee, by Charles Bird King. Thomas Gilcrease Institute of American History and Art.

Jesse Bushyhead, Cherokee, by Charles Bird King. Cherokee National Historical Society.

implements, and all other articles appertaining to Indian life and manners. . . ." Not only would such an arrangement "be productive of a happy effect on the imagination and disposition of the Indian deputations, which, from time to time, repair to Washington, and with which this Government transacts very important business," it would also "form a repository, possessing a high degree of scientific and historical value."[51]

Hezikiah Niles, editor of *Niles' Weekly Register,* was also amazed at McKenney's critics. "The 'Indian gallery,' at Washington," he wrote a few months later, "was, in the *uproar* about 'retrenchment and reform,' attacked by several ephemeras in and out of congress;— but, unless destroyed by fire or some other accident, it will remain as a monument to the *national honor* longer than a belief can be entertained that our country ever held things so mean as to snarl at the cost of collecting it."[52]

In any event, McKenney kept the gallery, but the use of public funds for portraits practically ceased. From the time the congressional report became public in May 1828 until he left office over two years later, McKenney spent only $219 for seven more paintings: $132 for five Winnebago portraits, $51 for a portrait of Red Jacket, and $20 for that of Mohongo, an Osage woman, and her child.

The Winnebago delegation came to Washington in the fall of 1828. When the delegates visited the Indian office, they were very impressed with the portrait gallery. They were particularly gratified, McKenney informed Secretary of War Peter B. Porter, "at seeing so many who were known to them." But they also said: *"We see no Winnebagoes here."* The colonel requested permission for King to paint a few Winnebago portraits for the gallery. Porter refused. A month later, as the delegation was preparing to leave the city, McKenney renewed his request. "The almost daily visits made to this office of these poor wanderers, the Winnebagoes, show an attachment so decided to the faces of those who have been painted, & that hang here; and they evince so much anxiety to have a similar respect paid to them, as to lead me to ask that you permit the likeness of Five of the principal men to be taken. . . . Yesterday they took off their bells, & ornaments, & caps, & gave me their war clubs requesting that *these* might hang up here as memorials." Porter at last consented and five Winnebago portraits were added to the gallery. Caleb Atwater, who later negotiated a treaty with the Winnebagos at Prairie du Chien, Wisconsin, recalled that "nothing pleased them so much as to tell them that their likenesses were in the War Department, and that their fame was spread through the world."[53]

King evidently was not as pleased, because the War Department was unusually slow in paying him for the portraits. On February 1, 1829, he sent them to McKenney with the following note: "Will you oblige me by placing the accompanying account in such a train that when the appropriation is made one visit to the Department will be sufficient? I hope the Portraits will please you." Instead of money, King received the Red Jacket commission. When more than three months passed without payment, the worried artist decided to prod McKenney. "I shall feel much obliged," he wrote, "if you will inform me what decision the Secretary of War has made on my account for Indian Portraits." Do not worry, McKenney responded. "The Secy of War agrees to pay the bill when the appropriation will permit it, & to add also the cost of the painting of Red Jacket, & to issue a new requisition for the whole in one bill."[54] Apparently this is how the matter was resolved because King did get paid for these portraits.

Generally, the Indians were on their best behavior while in the capital, but the sixteen members of the Winnebago delegation, when they were not having their portraits painted, appear to have been especially boisterous. Washington socialite Margaret Bayard Smith certainly did not appreciate their antics, particularly when several of the "ferocious Winnebagos," as she described them, took to grabbing and kissing passing ladies "till decent young women are afraid to walk out." Proclaiming herself a self-appointed representative of the women of Washington, she stormed into the secretary of war's office and demanded he do something about the Indians. Her mission was evidently successful but, as she later reported, "you have no idea, what a general dread they inspired."[55]

The ladies of Washington were not the only ones happy to see the Winnebagos leave. Joshua Tennison also heaved a sigh of relief as the Indians climbed aboard the stages waiting to take them home; that very afternoon he sent McKenney a bill for $250 to repair "damage to the house, bedding, carpeting, tables, &c."[56]

McKenney was dismissed from office in August 1830. Although he had done a creditable job as superintendent of Indian affairs, his editorial support for John C. Calhoun eight years earlier had earned him the enmity of Andrew Jackson, who became president in 1829. Old Hickory did not remove McKenney from office immediately, but the colonel knew his days as superintendent were numbered. Before he left office, McKenney sold to the War Department for $200 the items in the archives he owned personally.[57] He later claimed he wanted to prevent dispersal of the collection, but the truth was he sorely needed the money. McKenney may have been poor, but he left an important legacy—the first museum in the nation's capital.

Among those who admired his archives was Frances Trollope, the often caustic British traveler and recorder of American customs. "The Bureau for Indian affairs," she wrote in her *Domestic Manners of the Americans,* "contains a room of great interest; the walls are entirely covered with original portraits of all the chiefs who, from time to time, have come to negotiate with their great father, as they call the president. These portraits are by Mr. King, and, it cannot be doubted, are excellent likenesses, as are all the portraits I have ever seen from the hands of that gentleman." Besides the portraits, she reported, "the room [also] contains many specimens of . . . [Indian] ingenuity, and even of their taste. There is a glass case in the room, wherein are arranged specimens of worked muslin and other needlework, some very excellent handwriting, and many other little productions of male and female Indians, all proving clearly that they are perfectly capable of civilization."[58]

The Indian office collection had become such an attraction, in fact, that Jonathan Elliot gave it extensive coverage in his 1830 guide to Washington. Elliot realized that public interest in the archives was "already awakened," with many citizens and strangers calling to view "what stands alone in the world." Nevertheless, he still wished to publicize this important collection, especially the Indian portraits. "But for this gallery," he declared, "our posterity would ask in vain—*'what sort of a looking being was the red man of this country?'*

In vain would the inquirers be told to *read* descriptions of him—these never could satisfy. He must be *seen* to be known. Here then is a gift to posterity."[59]

Indeed it was. No one knew that better than the resourceful McKenney. Even before his dismissal from office, he had been hard at work perfecting a plan to publish the gallery, presumably with King's blessing. It was a feat that took the better part of two decades to accomplish. Nonetheless, the three-volume *History of the Indian Tribes of North America,* which he and James Hall published in Philadelphia between 1836 and 1844, has proven to be the gift to posterity that Elliot predicted.

IV

Indian History Published At Last

How long McKenney had been hoping and planning to have his gallery reproduced is not known. He may have had the idea as early as 1822, when he persuaded King to do the first portraits. One thing is certain: he had begun work on the project long before he left public office. His efforts primarily were to find a wealthy partner who could afford to finance the expensive effort. One prospective partner was Jared Sparks, editor and proprietor of the *North American Review,* who casually discussed with McKenney the possibility of publishing "the rare & curious" collection. The Philadelphia printer Samuel F. Bradford did even better. In September 1829 he actually offered McKenney a partnership for the publication of the portraits.

Bradford proposed a work of twenty numbers, each containing six portraits measuring eighteen by fourteen inches, the same as King's originals. A biographical and anecdotal sketch based on materials "of an *authentic* character" would accompany each portrait. McKenney's part of the bargain was to provide the text; Bradford would bear all printing and publication expenses; the profits would be shared equally. Those profits, McKenney thought, would be *"beyond calculation."* [60]

Such were the origins of McKenney and Hall's *History of the Indian Tribes of North America,* a monument of nineteenth-century art and anthropology, a complicated publishing project that ultimately involved a great many years, a great variety of people, and a great deal of money. Several of the factors prominent in the beginning prevailed until 1844, when the last number finally appeared. Bradford was only the first of many publishers, printers, artists, lithographers, and businessmen to recognize the importance of King's Indian portraits and to risk fortune and reputation on their potential value. Sparks was only the first of many of McKenney's friends whose financial or intellectual assistance the colonel tried to enlist for his scheme. McKenney himself could often revive the optimism he had felt at first when prospects were bright, but periods of pessimism followed inevitably, and by 1844 the originating genius was no longer associated with the project.

But in 1830—before his dismissal from the Indian office—McKenney was full of enthusiasm and plans. He sent a circular to government officials, asking for biographical information about various Indian leaders. He gave Bradford six of the portraits to be lithographed in Philadelphia. He foiled the attempts of other artists to copy King's work. He even acquired more portraits.

The opportunity to enlarge the gallery presented itself with the highly publicized arrival in Washington of a party of Osage Indians. Six of them had been taken to Europe in 1827 by an enterprising American who had exhibited the Indians for two years, then heartlessly abandoned them in France. Sent home by the French government in the spring of 1830, two of the Indians had died of smallpox aboard ship, and the survivors, including a woman named Mohongo and her child, were brought to Washington before their return to Missouri.

Immediately, McKenney asked for permission to have Mohongo's portrait painted. "Nothing seems to delight all the Indians so much as these portraits," he told the secretary of war. "You know I am for it—& her history is so interesting, as to make it desirable; & again we have none of the osage nation." The secretary of war replied, "If Mr. King will . . . introduce the child for the usual price $20 let the Lady's request be indulged." Although King should have been paid more for a double portrait, McKenney urged the artist to accept the commission. *"Better do it*—I think it may open the door, again, for more work. The gallery is growing daily, in popularity."[61]

McKenney soon discovered to his chagrin just how popular the gallery had become. Fewer than three weeks later two elderly and respected Washingtonians requested permission to copy King's paintings and exhibit them throughout the United States. Understandably startled by this potential threat to his own as yet unannounced plans, McKenney refused. The gallery was the property of the nation, he informed the petitioners, and could not be exploited for private benefit "unless it were connected with some great national object; . . . by uniting the Gallary with a work on the Aborigines of this Country, and descriptions, and history of the Tribes, and the individuals, that might be represented in the Gallary. An undertaking upon such a basis," he reasoned, "would be national."[62] What he had outlined, of course, was his own project.

The petitioners were not to be so easily denied. They wrote President Jackson that even monarchs allowed their subjects to view and copy national works of art. Thus, they sneered, "it is strange that a subordinate clerk should dare to refuse to permit the artists of the Republic to copy the public paintings for the gratification of all the Citizens who may be willing to pay the artists for their labour in copying them and who cannot conveniently come to the Seat of Government."[63] McKenney, however, made sure that no replies were sent back up the bureaucratic chain of command, and the matter ended.

Bradford, meanwhile, took the Indian portraits to Cephas G. Childs, who had recently opened a lithographic firm on Chestnut Street across from Independence Hall. Lithography was relatively new, but the technique offered several advantages over traditional wood or steel engravings. With a greasy crayon, the picture was drawn on a specially prepared stone. When the stone was dampened, the ink adhered only to the drawing. Thus the drawings could be made more quickly; correcting them was easier; and the stones were durable enough to provide hundreds of crisp, clear prints to be colored by hand. Although Childs was a skilled craftsman himself, the most gifted member of the firm was his deaf-mute apprentice Albert Newsam, whose specialty was copying oil portraits at a reduced size on stone; for twenty-five dollars the customer received the stone and twenty-five prints. To enhance the prestige of his firm, Childs soon convinced Henry Inman, the noted New York portrait painter, to become his partner. Now Childs and Inman, Lithographers, the firm moved to the southeast corner of Fifth and Walnut streets in Philadelphia.

When McKenney saw the first proofs of the Indian lithographs, he was amazed by their quality. "I consider the above copy, perfect; a perfect likeness of the man,

Mah.has.kah. Chief of
the Ioways. (White Cloud).

I consider the above copy, perfect; a perfect likeness of the
man, who is known to me — and an exact copy of the
original drawing by King, now in the office of Indian affairs.

Tho. L. McKenney

Dept. of War — Office In. Affrs
Apr 29. 1830.

who is known to me—and an exact copy of the original drawing by King, now in the office of Indian affairs," he noted on the margin of Mahaskah's lithograph.[64]

The partners felt confident enough by the middle of 1830 to announce publicly the plans for their "GREAT NATIONAL WORK." The prospectus promised 120 portraits printed on fine, heavy paper "corresponding to the value and size of the work, and to its intended perpetuity." In addition to a biographical sketch of each Indian portrayed, McKenney's text would consist of an essay "calculated to throw a light upon the history of this people." The price would be $6 a number or $120 for the entire set.

The project had barely been launched, however, when McKenney lost his job as superintendent of Indian affairs—the first in a nearly endless series of setbacks. The blow could have been fatal. McKenney lost control of the gallery, the library of books and manuscripts he had so diligently collected over the years, and the franking privilege as well. Nevertheless, McKenney was determined to see his project through to completion. He moved to Philadelphia, became a newspaper editor, and completed a rough draft of the introductory essay by the end of the year.

The first proof sheet of the history was printed in September 1831. Characteristically, McKenney turned to an acquaintance for help in correcting it. He appealed to former president John Quincy Adams, who was then living in Quincy, Massachusetts, for "the co-operating scrutiny of more gifted minds. I do this," he admitted, "because I distrust my own ability—& fear to venture forth until *the proofs,* at least, shall pass in review before some competent intelligence." Impressed with the work's magnitude and importance, Adams agreed to read the galleys, becoming, as a result, editor of the historical narrative. "I return herewith the proof sheet of the great work which you have undertaken," he replied, "and which I trust will survive the unfortunate race of men whom we are extinguishing with merciless rapidity."[65]

McKenney, isolated from the books and records in Washington, never hesitated to ask friends to supply elusive names, dates, and facts essential to his narrative. "I am puzzled about . . . that traveler," McKenney admitted to Adams, who had queried him about a missing name. "I have written to Gov Cass to look him up for me. If I fail to get him I shall have to modify the sentence but retain the *fact.*" The traveler's name—Jacques Cartier—came not from Adams or Cass but from Albert Gallatin, the financier and statesman, who furnished enough information "for a volume."[66]

Not only did McKenney's friends provide invaluable technical assistance, those in government helped finance his extensive correspondence by franking his mail. As he explained to Gallatin, "My postage is so considerable as to be an object with me to lessen it—and I have the privilege of using several of my friends in matters pertaining to my work in this way." This was only fair, he rationalized, since the history would be a contribution to the nation and "ought [to] be sustained more practically, & extensively than this."[67] His helpful friends included Adams, Cass, Richard M. Johnson of Kentucky, and Delegate Joseph M. White of Florida Territory.

His Philadelphia associates, McKenney felt, were less obliging. "Those printers are wonderful people," he complained to Adams. "I was promised two proofs in a

HISTORY

OF THE

INDIAN TRIBES

OF

NORTH AMERICA,

WITH

BIOGRAPHICAL SKETCHES AND ANECDOTES

OF THE

PRINCIPAL CHIEFS.

EMBELLISHED WITH 120 PORTRAITS,

From the Indian Gallery in the Department of War at Washington.

———

GREAT NATIONAL WORK.

The public are aware that a most interesting and curious collection of Indian portraits has been making since 1821, by the Executive of the United States; and that this collection forms a gallery in the Indian department at Washington, numbering at this time about one hundred and twenty heads. The interest felt in this effort to preserve the likenesses and costume of our aborigines—a work so intimately connected with the natural history of man, is indicated by the immense numbers of our citizens and foreigners, who visit this gallery; and the uniform admiration they express of its valuable and interesting character. Believing the public will sustain the undertaking, the undersigned has made arrangements for publishing this unique group. He accompanies this prospectus with a specimen of one head. It is a *fac simile,* as all the rest shall be. That nothing might be lost, the size of most of the original drawings has been preserved. The original drawings, it may be proper to remark, are principally by King, of Washington, from life; and will be vouched by responsible names, to be *perfect* likenesses.

The tribes represented in this gallery are eighteen in number, viz: Chippewas, (or Ojibwa,) Sioux, Menomone, Winnebago, Sauk, Fox, Oto, Panis, Maha, Kansas, Seneca, Shawanee, Delaware, Creek, (or Muscogee,) Uchee, Cherokee, Choctaws, (or Chata,) and Seminole.

Hopes are entertained, that a likeness of the celebrated Pocahontas, and of Captain John Smith, from original drawings, known to be in the Bowling family, in Virginia, will accompany the publication.

It is proposed to publish the work in twenty numbers, each number to contain six heads. The impression will be on fine thick paper, corresponding to the value and size of the work, and to its intended perpetuity.

An essay suited to such a work, and calculated to throw a light upon the history of this interesting people, will accompany the first number; and as materials will authorize it, the remaining numbers will be interspersed with biographical sketches, and anecdotes of the originals, and with vocabularies.

This division of the undertaking will be executed by Col. M'Kenney of the Indian department, whose long and familiar acquaintance with our Indian relations, and travels over the country inhabited by most of the tribes, and personal acquaintance with most of the originals, authorize the conclusion, that what he may furnish will not only be a suitable accompaniment for such a work, but add greatly to its interest and value.

A map of the country will be carefully prepared, and the location of the several tribes represented in the publication, noted upon it.

The undersigned believes that there nowhere exists such materials for a work so unique, so interesting, and in all that regards the aborigines of America, so authentic and instructive. Its great value as it regards the United States, can be appreciated properly, perhaps, only by posterity, because the Indians, though thinned and scattered, are yet among us. Europe, it is believed, is prepared now to put the proper estimate upon the work. In order, therefore, that countries other than our own, may enjoy the gratification of beholding the red men of our forests, in their almost breathing likenesses, and in their native, and varied, and singular costumes, arrangements will be made for publishing the work, simultaneously, in Europe.

The price to subscribers for each number will be six dollars, to be paid on delivery.

The undersigned avails himself of the following flattering notice of this design, in a letter from Dr. Sparks, editor of the North American Review, to Col. M'Kenney. From a gentleman so distinguished as Doctor Sparks, so well, and so deservedly appreciated for his high standing, attainments, his taste and science, and with such enlarged opportunities of judging of the importance of such a work, such a letter is very encouraging.

"Boston, September 27, 1829.

"My dear sir,

"I am heartily rejoiced to learn by your favour of the 22nd instant, that there is so good a prospect for publishing the portraits of the red men. I do not consider that I have any claim, growing out of our conversation, and, indeed, as my only motive was to be instrumental in bringing before the public, so rare and curious a collection, it is a double satisfaction for me to know, that the matter is in so good hands, and encourages hopes of entire success. Mr. Bradford has enterprise and skill in this business, and if he takes hold of it heartily, the thing is done. In my mind, the whole glory and value of the undertaking, will depend on the accuracy and beauty, with which the heads shall be executed, and the completeness of the costume. You must write all that is known about the character and life of each person. Let us have a work worthy of the subject, and honourable to the nation, and just to the Indians.

"Very sincerely your friend and obedient servant,

(Signed) "Jared Sparks."

Th. L. M'Kenney, Esq.

The undersigned assures the public that it is his full intention to make the work an ornament to the arts, and worthy of the nation.

Samuel F. Bradford.

Philadelphia, October 11, 1830.

week, and find it impossible to get but one—the reason assigned, is, 'The Type being scarce, and another 'job' coming in, part is taken up with that!' There is nothing like patience," he lamented. "I try, under all the circumstances of my case, to exercise what I possess, and often wish I had a larger stock."[68]

Hints of pessimism appeared in McKenney's correspondence in May 1832. He explained to Nicholas Biddle, a subscriber, why the publication had been so delayed. Obtaining biographical information about the Indians was proving to be much more difficult than he had anticipated. "The very elements are scarcely less variable, or more difficult to grasp, than are those Indians, and the incidents of their lives," he declared. The most critical problem was financial. Despite McKenney's claim that "few works ever received a patronage more extensive, or more honorable," he admitted that subscriptions would not be enough to sustain the project.[69] McKenney's estimate was correct; Bradford went bankrupt before the end of the year, the first financial casualty of the Indian history.

With McKenney, however, gloom could not last. Recalling Jared Sparks's earlier interest in the paintings, McKenney again offered the scholar the opportunity of joining the project and writing the biographies. Buy Bradford out, McKenney pleaded in April 1833. The cost would be minimal. The printer wanted only to be reimbursed for his expenses thus far. McKenney even offered to share future expenditures, assuring Sparks that credit could be had on everything—engravings, paper, and printing—and thus the work would pay for itself as each succeeding number appeared. *"A fortune* awaits us," McKenney exclaimed.[70]

Sparks was intrigued and asked for more information. A grim picture emerged from McKenney's reply. In almost four years, only a dozen portraits had been lithographed. For these, however, the entire edition of 400 copies had been struck. The fifty-four folio pages of the historical narrative intended for the first number had also been printed, but not a single biography. One was almost written, and there was material for perhaps five or six others. To obtain enough biographical information for all the Indians someone would have to make a research trip through the West. "This you can make, or we can get Cass to send Schoolcraft [an Indian agent] through the Country on *other* business" and, through him, "get all we may want." For the first number, including the narrative, $1,250 had been spent, almost half on coloring the portraits. Although there were only 104 subscribers, McKenney held out hopes for a large European market.

The portraits, of course, were the key to the success of the venture, and only McKenney would have permission to reproduce the War Department gallery. His friend Cass, now secretary of war, had given his personal *"assurance"* on that point. The president could overrule Cass, but McKenney had shrewdly protected himself by having Inman copy in oil each Indian portrait as it arrived from Washington. The effect of the thirty or forty already finished, McKenney claimed, "is more impressive than any thing I ever saw. Inman you know is a Master—& his reputation is staked on his success." By fall, McKenney promised, *"all will be in my hands."* The lithographs could then be made from Inman's copies "at leisure" and "thus *secure* the prize."[71]

Sparks failed to reply, but Edward C. Biddle and John Key, two young Philadelphia printers, bought Bradford out and saved the project. Not only did they agree

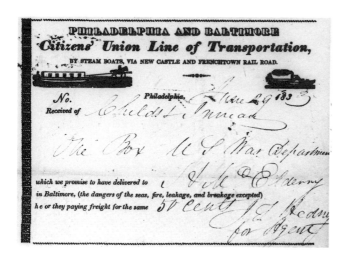

to continue the Indian history, they also accepted Bradford's original contract: they would bear all expenses as publishers, McKenney would provide the copy. Someone, however, still had to make a trip west, a trip McKenney could not make because of his newspaper responsibilities. After only two weeks, he again wrote Sparks, this time offering to make him "joint editor." Sparks had only to "go to Washington, lay the foundation for materials, work them up—go, if necessary, West . . . and share with me my half of the proceeds of the work."[72] The scholar ignored this letter as well.

Fortunately, Nathan Sargent, publisher of McKenney's paper, agreed to make the trip. McKenney had Sargent apply to Cass for letters of introduction to Indian agents, and Cass referred the request to Commissioner of Indian Affairs Elbert Herring, who promptly proved himself as true a friend as Cass. "As the work will be of great interest and read with avidity, it is important that the facts contained in it should be authentic, and the information respecting the tribes and individuals full and satisfactory," Herring wrote several of his most knowledgeable and experienced agents. "It would therefore be gratifying to the Department, if you would be pleased to comply with Mr. Sargent's request, and furnish him in the way proposed with such particulars . . . as may be in your power to give."[73]

Other phases of the project also resumed in the following months. Before the end of 1833, Inman copied some fifty-five more portraits. McKenney or his associates had been carrying the paintings back and forth between Washington and Philadelphia, but now the accelerated pace dictated the use of commercial conveyance. Freight charges were ridiculously cheap; two boxes, each containing five portraits, were shipped in June for only 62½ cents. Inevitably, one box went astray, although the errant portraits were later found. Herring ruled, however, that future shipments could not be sent by railway express.

More than ever, the project depended on the tolerance of McKenney's friends in the government, and certainly his demands must have strained the best of friendships. McKenney complained impatiently to Cass when paintings did not arrive speedily. He asked for portraits that could not be found. He once sent a set of lithographs to the Indian office so that Hezikiah Miller, his former copy clerk, could identify the Indians. "The *stupe* of a Lithographist forgot to inscribe the names," McKenney wrote. Incredibly, a month later he asked the commissioner to have Miller, "whose pen is always ready in a good cause," make a duplicate set of the names because McKenney had mislaid the first.[74]

These were minor troubles compared to the project's second major setback: the collapse of Childs and Inman, Lithographers. Childs had lured the prominent artist to Philadelphia with the promise of numerous commissions in oil, anticipating a lively trade from patrons who would have their portraits painted, in Inman's second-floor studio, and then lithographed. Except for a few important orders, notably the portrait of John Marshall commissioned by the Philadelphia Bar Association, the partnership never fulfilled its promise, and the firm dissolved. Before his return to New York, however, Inman had copied in oil more than one hundred portraits from the War Department Indian gallery.

Childs promptly found a new partner, the landscape artist George Lehman, who had been working with the firm since 1830. As Childs and Lehman, the company struggled another year until Childs himself withdrew. Heavily in debt, he considered his lithographic career a failure. To the faithful Newsam he owed $50, an obligation that remained unpaid for eleven years; to his printer, P. S. Duval, whom he had brought from France in 1831, he owed a staggering $750. Childs and Lehman became Lehman and Duval; the talented Newsam remained with the new firm.

A thoroughly discouraged McKenney temporarily shelved the project and spent a fruitless two years working for the Whig party of Pennsylvania. This political odyssey cost him the support of Nathan Sargent, who had long since thought better of his agreement with the colonel, and of John Key, who was about to withdraw from his partnership with Edward Biddle.

To compound his problems, McKenney now also faced the challenge of a competing Indian portfolio. His erstwhile traveling companion, James Otto Lewis, beat McKenney to press with a project of his own. The obscure Detroit artist was evidently embittered by the well-publicized plan to publish the War Department gallery. More than one-third of the paintings were based on his original drawings, yet he would receive neither recognition nor recompense.

Clutching his portfolio of watercolors, Lewis went to Philadelphia in search of a publisher—and found Lehman and Duval. Why McKenney's lithographers accepted a job that would undercut him is a mystery. The struggling craftsmen may have needed the business; perhaps they considered McKenney's venture a lost cause. Whatever the reason, the first number of Lewis's *Aboriginal Port-Folio* appeared in June 1835. Succeeding numbers of the ill-advised and hurriedly done project appeared irregularly over the next few months. Although Lewis had planned to publish eighty lithographs in ten numbers, the total produced was seventy-two. At two dollars a number, the *Aboriginal Port-Folio* was cheaper than McKenney's planned work, but the quality of the lithographs was vastly inferior. Biographical sketches probably accompanied at least a few of the first numbers, but none are known to be extant. Most copies of the *Port-Folio* also lacked title page and text other than a sheet entitled: "Advertisement to the First Number of *The Aboriginal Port-Folio*."

This advertisement, however, plainly shows that Lewis hoped to disrupt McKenney's publishing plans. "In presenting the first number of the following work to the public," Lewis wrote, "the publisher will perhaps be excused for candidly acknowledging the consciousness of his own inability to render that full justice in its execution, which the subject from its own importance requires; but as the present is the *first* attempt of the kind in this country, he sincerely trusts, that the judicious and critical will regard it with a favorable and indulgent eye. . . . Copies from the principal *originals* were painted by Mr. King, of Washington, and are now deposited in the War Office."

ADVERTISEMENT

TO THE

FIRST NUMBER

OF THE

ABORIGINAL PORT-FOLIO.

In presenting the first Number of the following work
to the public, the Publisher will, perhaps, be excused
for candidly acknowledging the consciousness of his own
inability to render that full justice in its execution, which
the subject from its own importance requires; but as the
present is the *first* attempt of the kind in this country,
he sincerely trusts, that the judicious and critical will
regard it with a favourable and indulgent eye.

The great and constantly recurring disadvantages to
which an artist is necessarily subject, while travelling
through a wilderness, far removed from the abodes of
civilization, and in "pencilling by the way," with the
rude materials he may be enabled to pick up in the
course of his progress, will, he hopes, secure for him
the approbation, not only of the critic, but of the con-
noisseur:---And when it is recollected, that the time for
holding Indian treaties is generally very limited; that
the deep-felt anxiety of the artist to possess a large collection must be no small impediment in the way of his
bestowing any considerable share of his time and attention on any one production, together with the rapidity
with which he is obliged to labor; he confidently believes
as they are issued in their original state, that, whatever
imperfections may be discoverable, will be kindly as-
cribed to the proper and inevitable cause.

He would beg leave, moreover, to state, that he had
the honor to be employed by the Indian Department ex-
pressly for the purpose. As regards the merits of their
general character, and the fidelity of the costume, he can
with confidence assure the public, that the resemblances
of both are faithfully and accurately given.

Copies from the principal *originals* were painted by
Mr. King of Washington, and are now deposited in the
War Office. With this brief introduction, the Subscriber respectfully offers the work to the kind patronage
of his fellow citizens and the public.

J. O. LEWIS.

Philadelphia, July 20, 1835.

What McKenney and King thought of Lewis's effort is not known. Henry R. Schoolcraft, the Michigan Indian agent who knew Lewis well and had been on some of the trips when the sketches were made, considered the *Aboriginal Port-Folio* an important work. "Few artists have had his means of observation of the aboriginal man, in the great panorama of the West, where . . . [Lewis] has carried his easel," Schoolcraft noted in his diary. Perhaps the work was not "all that is desirable or practicable," but it deserved patronage "as a first and original effort" and "we should cherish all such efforts."[75]

Few Americans shared Schoolcraft's opinion of the *Port-Folio;* sales were so poor that today the lithographs are rare and valued collector's items. The *Port-Folio* is important to the present study, however, because at least five of King's surviving Indian portraits are based on Lewis models. Since none of the original Lewis drawings are extant, the lithographs in his *Port-Folio* must be presumed to be fairly accurate representations of his work. By comparing his portrait of Wanata, or The Charger, with King's version, Lewis's limited ability becomes obvious. In this case, King followed rather carefully the ethnological and artistic features of the Lewis original. Presumably, King exercised the same care in his other renderings of Lewis sketches.

Perhaps the challenge of Lewis's *Port-Folio* rekindled McKenney's optimism. To respond effectively he needed a partner with money, and for once he was lucky. James Hall of Cincinnati, Ohio, a prominent jurist and a prolific writer, agreed to the same terms that McKenney had originally offered Sparks. Hall was to do the writing; Biddle, who agreed to carry on alone as publisher, would bear all expenses. As Hall explained to the artist George Catlin, whom he unsuccessfully tried to lure into the partnership, the work would now be known as McKenney and Hall's *History of the Indian Tribes of North America,* but would still be published in twenty numbers, each consisting of six portraits and twenty or thirty pages of letterpress text. A portion of the text would be a general history, the remainder biographies of the Indians portrayed. "My materials for this part of the work are very voluminous, and of the most authentic character," the judge declared, "having been collected from a great number of the Indian agents and other gentlemen who are personally acquainted with the Indians."[76] Hall promptly left Cincinnati, arriving in Philadelphia early in February 1836.

"I became editor," Hall later wrote, "and set to work, with my usual ardor and energy (which were not small)." To his dismay, he discovered that the promised hoard of reference materials did not exist; after exhausting what little there was, he could not prevail on McKenney to gather more or to help with the writing. "I went on alone," he claimed. "The labor was Herculean. Here were a long list of Indian heroes, to be supplied with biographies—of whom we knew nothing but the names." For the next eight years, he corresponded and talked with Indian agents, traders, and soldiers, gleaned facts from the accounts of western travelers and examined and compared testimony. "I claim therefore that this work is not only full of new and interesting facts," Hall later wrote, "but that it is strictly reliable."[77]

Inspired by his new partner, McKenney resumed work on the project. He asked Commissioner Herring for six more Indian portraits and turned them over to the lithographers Lehman and Duval, who also resumed work—doubtless on credit. "I am glad you are through your apprehensions," McKenney wrote the partners, "& can go on faster."[78] The publisher, Biddle, began advertising the work in earnest, replacing the prospectus with pamphlets which urged potential subscribers to visit his shop where they could compare specimen lithographs with the Inman paintings. McKenney was also successful in selling the rights to publish the work in Great Britain to James M. Campbell. The British edition, however, was never completed.

The first number of McKenney and Hall's *History of the Indian Tribes of North America,* the culmination of eight years of effort, was published in February 1837. Biddle deposited one copy with the district court, thereby securing copyright. Three days later, on March 3, McKenney presented another copy, inscribed "from the authors & publisher," to the American Philosophical Society. Other copies went to newspapers and magazines for review. Everyone who saw it was impressed. "In all the mechanical departments the work, so far as published, is faultless," reported the *Philadelphia Saturday News*. The *Harrisburg Chronicle* thought the paintings had been "lithographed with great elegance, and coloured in a manner which has never been equalled this side of the Atlantic." The *Boston Daily Advertiser and Patriot* correctly predicted the work would be "a source of pleasure" to any subscriber and "a valuable legacy to his children."[79]

With such favorable publicity, it is not surprising that the *History* received a substantial patronage. "Its success is wonderful," McKenney wrote Sparks in May 1838. "Over 200.000$ sold; and about 70.000$ of that within the last four months and a half—30.000$ of this in New Orleans. Were the money sluices open, it would swell out to ½ a million, as I believe."[80] McKenney had not curbed his propensity for exaggeration, but his figures were close. The subscription book, now in the custody of the New York Public Library, lists approximately 1,250 subscribers, which meant an anticipated income of $150,000.

To all outward appearances, these were troublefree days for the project; succeeding numbers of the *History* appeared almost monthly. An ominous sign, however, was the withdrawal of Lehman and Duval from the enterprise in August 1837 after publication of the sixth number. They were replaced by J. T. Bowen of New York, who immediately transferred his business to Philadelphia, bringing with him Alfred Hoffy, who succeeded Newsam in the work of drawing the plates.

Bowen worked on a far grander scale than the previous lithographers. At his shop on Walnut Street, he at times employed as many as forty people on the McKenney and Hall project alone; twenty-five of them were women who did nothing but color the prints.[81] Lehman and Duval had drawn a half dozen or so illustrations for numbers seven and eight; Bowen printed and colored these and made six additional plates for the two numbers which completed volume one. Of the forty-eight plates in the initial volume, Childs and Inman provided three, Lehman and Duval thirty-nine, and Bowen six. Bowen, however, provided all the plates for volumes two and three, and later reissued volume one, deleting the names of his predecessors.

Mohongo and child, Osage, by Charles Bird King. Thornton Boileau.

Hoowaunneka [Little Elk], Winnebago, by Charles Bird King. Peabody Museum, Harvard University.

HOO-WAEI-NEE-KAW or LITTLE ELK,
of the Car-ray-mau-nee family.
— Winnebago Orator. —

Philadelphia Published by S.F.Bradford 181 Chesnut Street.
From Childs & Inman Press.

Left: This uncolored lithograph of Hoowaunneka [Little Elk] is the only one known to bear the firm name of S. F. Bradford, McKenney's first publisher. It was based on King's portrait of Little Elk, not Henry Inman's, and was never published. The published lithograph of Little Elk, like most of the others in the McKenney and Hall volumes, was taken from the Inman copy. Rare Book Division, The New York Public Library, Lenox and Tilden Foundations.

■ **Below:** Left, Hoowaunneka [Little Elk] by Henry Inman. Peabody Museum, Harvard University. ■ Right, the Hoowaunneka lithograph in McKenney and Hall's *History of the Indian Tribes of North America.* Unlike King's original portraits, most of the oil copies by Inman made for the McKenney and Hall project survived. Before 1843 McKenney promoted several schemes to raise capital by exhibiting the Inman paintings in Europe and selling them there. "I have been told that the strife between Noblemen for a collection of *such paintings* . . . would run it up to an enormous sum—not less in any body's estimation, than 100,000$," he wrote. McKenney's plans came to nothing, and ultimately the portraits passed into the hands of Tileston and Hollingsworth, a Boston paper company, in payment of a debt. In 1882 the paintings were given to Harvard's Peabody Museum of Archaeology and Ethnology.

HOO.WAN.NE.KA,
A WINNEBAGO CHIEF.

PUBLISHED BY J.T. BOWEN, PHILADA.

Left, Wanata [The Charger], Sioux, by Charles Bird King after James Otto Lewis. Gulf States Paper Corporation. ■ Right, Wanata [The Charger], lithograph in James Otto Lewis's *Aboriginal Port-Folio*. Library of Congress.

Although the change of lithographers seemed painless, the project was foundering. Seven numbers had been published in 1837, but only three appeared in 1838. In November Biddle withdrew as publisher, although he remained with the enterprise as its business agent. His place was taken by Frederick W. Greenough of Philadelphia. Unfortunately, changes of management could not solve the principal problem, the depression that followed the panic of 1837. Particularly hard hit were southern planters, merchants, and financiers—a group which made up over half the subscription list. "Embarrassments thickened over the land," McKenney explained, ". . . whilst many of the subscribers who were rich when they patronized the work, failed, or changed their residence, or died. Under such circumstances," he sighed, "were my cherished hopes crushed."[82]

Frustrated and bitter, McKenney became completely estranged from the project. "It seems an age since I have conversed with you," Biddle wrote him in April 1841. "Do drop me a few lines to let me know your whereabouts & inform me of your prospects. Many anxious enquiries are made by those who feel interested in your welfare; & I regret that I am unable to satisfy them."[83]

Bowen waited almost two years for the publishers to recover financially, then he resumed the project alone in an attempt to recoup something for the costly lithographic services he had provided on credit. In December 1841 he published number fourteen and was immediately challenged by Biddle, who claimed that the lithographer had acted without authority. Biddle asked all subscribers not to pay for copies that were delivered. The controversy was not resolved until the following October when Biddle and Bowen agreed to transfer their publication rights to the Philadelphia printers Daniel Rice and James G. Clark, the assignees of the now bankrupt Greenough. As a result, Rice and Clark became the fifth and final publishers of McKenney and Hall's *History of the Indian Tribes of North America*. As James Hall later commented, the project was now in the hands of "a couple of Yankees."[84]

While McKenney went his separate way, the new publishers, with Hall and Bowen, pushed the Indian history to completion. In July 1842 they asked the War Department for the loan of Wakechai's portrait and during that year succeeded in publishing numbers fifteen and sixteen. The last number appeared in January 1844, some fifteen years after the project began.

McKenney and Hall's *History of the Indian Tribes of North America* was an artistic and technological achievement which established J. T. Bowen as the country's finest lithographer and proved that American lithography could rival the best European products. Its success encouraged John James Audubon, the great naturalist, to contract with Bowen to provide illustrations for a revised edition of *Birds of America* to sell in the United States at $100 in contrast to the prohibitive $1,000 of the English edition. As a Philadelphia reviewer pointed out, "Audubon was truly fortunate in placing his great work in such hands, but he had seen the Indians and their admirable execution."[85]

Bowen may have realized immediate fruits from the Indian history, but the project never reaped for McKenney the material benefit he so desperately desired. Nor did the authors gain fame for their efforts. "The large and expensive form of the

Authorized subscription agents for the *History of the Indian Tribes of North America,* taken from an original wrapper for one of the volume numbers. American Philosophical Society.

AGENTS

FOR

THE INDIAN BIOGRAPHY.

MAINE.

Bangor, Duren & Thatcher.

MASSACHUSETTS.

Boston, William D. Ticknor.

RHODE ISLAND.

Providence, John E. Brown.

CONNECTICUT.

Hartford, Spalding & Storrs.
New Haven, Durrie & Peck.

NEW YORK.

New York, Scofield & Voorhies.
Rochester, Hoyt, Porter & Co.
Albany, Oliver Steele.
Buffalo,

PENNSYLVANIA.

Harrisburg, J. & F. Wyeth.
Lancaster, Mrs. Mary Dickson, P. M.
Pittsburg, Charles H. Kay.

DELAWARE.

Wilmington, Peter B. Porter.

MARYLAND.

Baltimore, N. Hickman.

DISTRICT OF COLUMBIA.

Washington, Franck Taylor.

VIRGINIA.

Richmond, Smith & Palmer.
Wheeling, Robert Fisher.
Norfolk, C. Bonsal.
Fredericksburg, John Coakley.

NORTH CAROLINA.

Fayetteville, E. J. Hale.
Raleigh, Turner & Hughes.

SOUTH CAROLINA.

Charleston, S. Babcock & Co.
Columbia, W. Cunningham.

GEORGIA.

Savannah, W. Thorne Williams.
Augusta, T. H. & I. C. Plant.
Columbus, I. C. Plant & Co.

ALABAMA.

Mobile, J. S. Kellogg & Co.

MISSISSIPPI.

Natchez, N. L. Williams.
Vicksburg,

LOUISIANA.

New Orleans, Norman, Steel & Co.

MISSOURI.

St. Louis, J. C. Dinnies & Co.

KENTUCKY.

Louisville, Morton & Griswold.
Lexington, A. T. Skillman.
Frankfort, C. H. Julian.
Maysville, Edward Cox.

TENNESSEE.

Nashville, W. A. Eichbaum.
Memphis, Folkes & Pugh.

OHIO.

Cincinnati, Alexander Flash.
Columbus, Isaac N. Whiting.

ILLINOIS.

Chicago, S. F. Gale.

MICHIGAN.

Detroit, J. S. & S. A. Bagg.

UPPER CANADA.

Montreal, William Greig.

work ($120 for the whole)," Hall later complained, "has confined it to public libraries, or to the collections of wealthy persons, so that it is not known in the literature of the country, nor has it gained me any reputation. But it is the most authentic work on the subject." Indeed, historians and anthropologists owe McKenney a debt of gratitude. A less visionary man would never have begun the mammoth, tremendously expensive project, attempting on such a grand scale a venture barely feasible technologically. The judgment of the *Saturday Courier* that the Indian history is "one of the largest and most splendid works which the literature and arts of the country have ever produced" is as true today as it was in 1842. [86]

V

The Gallery Continues To Grow

Although McKenney left office in 1830, for more than a decade King continued to paint portraits of Indians visiting Washington. The exact number of these portraits is unknown, certainly no more than thirty. The War Department commissioned most of them, although King did a few voluntarily, either as a favor to McKenney or as an artistic exercise of his own. These include his portraits of The Light, an Assiniboin visitor of 1831, and Black Hawk, the Sac chief who came to Washington two years later as a prisoner of war. Neither of these portraits was part of the War Department collection and neither was reproduced in the McKenney and Hall volumes.

The portraits of Chenannoquot and Amiskquew, two Menominee visitors to Washington in the winter of 1830, were the first King did after McKenney left office. Although this commission is not mentioned in federal records, at least one of the portraits—Amiskquew's—was in the War Department gallery, which indicates they were part of the regular series. Perhaps the best evidence is a note King sent to the commissioner of Indian affairs, "asking the loan of Indian portraits for the purpose of taking copies," a few days after the Menominees left Washington.[87]

The Menominees, an Algonquin tribe whose name is derived from the Chippewa word for wild rice, still live in Wisconsin near Green Bay where the first white explorers found them in 1634. A generally peaceful people, the Menominees subsisted primarily on game and the wild rice that grew abundantly in the shallow lakes and rivers around Green Bay. They bothered no one and asked little of others except to be left alone. Hence, the Menominees had reason to be angry when, in the 1820s, the government asked them to make room for several eastern tribes—the Stockbridges, Munsees, and Oneidas of New York—dislocated as a result of the Indian removal program. The government made several unsuccessful attempts to reconcile the tribe to its new neighbors; McKenney himself visited the Menominees in 1827, but the treaty of Butte des Morts, which they signed on that occasion, did little to resolve the basic discontent.

Three years later, as a last resort, the Menominee agent, Samuel C. Stambaugh, asked President Andrew Jackson for permission to bring a delegation to Washington. According to Stambaugh, "the *peace,* happiness, and prosperity of this interesting section of country" depended on allowing the Menominee leaders to "see their great Father the President of the United States, and make known to him, in *their own way,* separate & apart from *improper* interference, their views & wishes in relation to their disputes with the New York Indians; which is now costing the government, annually, large sums of money, without producing any beneficial effects to either of the parties concerned." The secretary of war at first turned down the request, claiming insufficient funds to cover the cost, but Stambaugh persisted and soon left for Washington with fourteen Menominee chiefs and warriors.

The delegates, "as an evidence of their love and veneration for their Great Father," resolved their difficulties and signed a treaty on February 8, 1831, permitting the New York Indians to occupy Menominee land. "Chi-mi-na-na-quet, [the] great cloud," was one of twelve Menominee signatories. Amiskquew was one of two who refused to sign.[88]

A few months after the Menominees left, their places were taken by a delegation from the Upper Missouri, 2,000 miles upriver from St. Louis. Never before had Indians from that region toured the East. The tribes the four delegates represented—Assiniboin, Cree, Plains Ojibwa, and Yanktonai Sioux—controlled some of the richest fur resources of the Far West.[89] Government officials, prodded by John Jacob Astor, president of the American Fur Company, felt these militant tribes should get a taste of civilization. Perhaps they would then become more cooperative in their dealings with representatives of the United States. As their agent, Major John F. A. Sanford, described his charges, they were "the most hostile and most remote of the Indians with whom our Citizens have intercourse, their trade the most valuable and constantly increasing." But, he pointed out, "they are beyond the reach of punishment or hope of presents."[90]

Accordingly, the secretary of war in the fall of 1831 authorized Sanford to bring a delegation to Washington. The agent, two interpreters, and the four intrepid warriors began the long and dangerous trip in early November from Fort Union at the mouth of the Yellowstone, near the present Montana-North Dakota line. Some six weeks later they arrived in St. Louis where they met George Catlin, just beginning his career as a chronicler of the life and culture of the American Indian. The young artist seized the opportunity to paint portraits of two of the delegates: the Assiniboin Wijunjon, or The Light, whom Catlin mistakenly identified as Pigeon Eggs Head, and his Cree companion, Broken Arm. After spending several weeks in St. Louis regaining their strength for the overland journey to Washington, getting vaccinated against the dreaded smallpox, and adjusting to the new foods and climate, the delegates left for the capital on New Year's Day, arriving two weeks later.

The Light was the star attraction. Handsome, tall, garbed in decorated buckskins, the friendly Assiniboin was a born showman who quickly stole the limelight from his shyer companions. At their meeting with the Great Father, he gave President Jackson an Indian name and his finest buckskin suit; Old Hickory, in return, presented him with a general's uniform as well as the customary peace medal.

The Light evidently also struck the fancy of Charles Bird King, because the artist added his portrait to his private collection. At least, the portrait does not appear to have been part of the War Department gallery, which indicates it was not commissioned by the government. King also evidently captioned the portrait at a much later date, entitling it: "Assiniboin Indian, from the most remote tribe that had ever visited Washington up to 1838." The portrait, however, is not one of King's better efforts and suffers in comparison with Catlin's.

Following the typical whirlwind tour of the East, the four visitors were soon on their way home. The cost of the delegation had been $6,450, including $1,000 for

presents. When questioned on the large sum spent for gifts, Sanford responded: "Without presents they have no ears."[91]

In St. Louis arrangements were made for the delegation to return to Fort Union aboard the American Fur Company steamboat *Yellowstone,* making her maiden voyage. A fellow passenger, by coincidence, was Catlin. The change in appearance and demeanor of The Light, who haughtily paraded the decks in his military regalia, so struck the artist that he painted a second portrait. This one has two full-length views: one as the noble warrior appeared en route to Washington, the other as he looked upon his return. Catlin's dismay is obvious. The Light sports a fan, umbrella, and white gloves; a pair of ill-concealed whiskey bottles peek from beneath the tails of his greatcoat.

Catlin was not alone in his dismay. The Light's fellow tribesmen also disapproved of the changes in their representative. They were annoyed not only at his arrogance but also at his fantastic tales about the strange and marvelous things he had seen in the East. All that saved him from instant disaster was the belief of his fellow Assiniboins that he had special powers protecting him from ordinary lead bullets. This tolerance, however, ended the night the former delegate described the Baltimore shot tower to a group of disbelieving companions, who openly hooted at the story of a building so tall. Disgusted, The Light broke his prized umbrella over the back of one particularly obnoxious heckler and stalked off into the darkness. The heckler, in turn, fashioned a bullet from iron—just in case The Light did have magical powers—and went looking for him. He found him sulking in his tent before the fire and shot off the top of his head.

Perhaps the most celebrated Indian visitor to Washington in this period was Black Hawk, captured in 1832 after a brief but futile attempt to retain his Illinois homeland. It had not been much of a war. The only major engagement, the so-called Battle of the Bad Axe, had been little more than a massacre of Black Hawk's dispirited Sac and Fox followers. After imprisonment at Jefferson Barracks in St. Louis, Black Hawk, his son, and

Opposite: Left, The Light [Wijunjon], Assiniboin, by Charles Bird King. Gulf States Paper Corporation. ■ Right, The Light, by George Catlin. National Collection of Fine Arts, Smithsonian Institution. ■ **Below:** The Light, going to and returning from Washington, by George Catlin. National Collection of Fine Arts, Smithsonian Institution.

four followers were sent east to a safer prison. In April 1833 they reached Washington, where they had a cordial meeting with President Jackson. From the White House they went next door to the War Department and saw the King gallery. "They expressed more surprise and pleasure at the portraits," wrote an observer, "than at anything else that was shown them in Washington, recognizing many of them."[92]

During this visit Black Hawk sat for the portrait by King that appears in this book. Like the portrait of The Light, this one was not done at War Department request. Indeed, McKenney himself may have suggested it, because, in a letter to Jared Sparks written in late April, he claimed to have "a noble drawing of Black Hawk" which was not in the gallery at Washington. Inexplicably, however, McKenney later that year twice asked the commissioner of Indian affairs to send King's painting, prompting this response: "The likeness of Black Hawk is not in the Indian Office, nor has it ever been taken by order of the Department and cannot therefore be forwarded by me."[93] As a result, the lithographed likeness of Black Hawk that McKenney eventually published in his *History of the Indian Tribes of North America* was not taken from this portrait, but from another one of the Sac chief that King did during a subsequent visit to Washington.

The Indians were in prison only a month or so, at Fortress Monroe in Norfolk, Virginia, when Secretary of War Cass decided it was safe for them to return to the Midwest. To ensure their rehabilitation, the prisoners went home by way of Baltimore, Philadelphia, New York, Albany, and the Great Lakes so that they could see firsthand the power of the Long Knives. Accordingly, the prisoners visited a bewildering array of military facilities and public buildings, including the seventy-four-gun battleship *Delaware* and the Philadelphia mint. Everywhere the warriors went, however, crowds of curiosity seekers swarmed to meet them, treating them more like conquering heroes than prisoners of war. Several women kissed Whirling Thunder, Black Hawk's son, described as a "noble specimen of physical beauty"; a New Yorker gave the old chief earrings for his wife. At Albany the crowd was so thick the prisoners could not get off their boat for over an hour after it docked.

One of the citizens most anxious to see Black Hawk was McKenney, hard at work on his *History* when the Sac chief was passing through Philadelphia. McKenney requested a private meeting with the celebrated warrior "of some few hours" for acquiring information not only about him but also about "other Indians with whom he may be acquainted." Accordingly, Cass instructed the army officer conducting the chief on his eastern tour to "to accommodate Col. McKenney in this particular, and to direct the Interpreter . . . to accompany Black Hawk."[94]

Four years later, Black Hawk was back in Washington, this time as part of an ambitious government effort to bring peace between the Sac and Fox and their mortal enemies, the Santee or Minnesota Sioux. The hatred was so intense, an Indian agent informed the secretary of war, that the Sac and Fox would agree to anything "except to *love* a Sioux, or spare his life if they met him in the wild prairies and have the opportunity to scalp him."[95] An uneasy peace prevailed until the spring of 1837 when a Sioux war party collected twenty Sac and Fox scalps. The outraged Sac and Fox immediately sent war belts to their Winnebago, Iowa, Oto, Pawnee, and Omaha neighbors in an attempt to enlist their help

Makataimeshekiakiah [Black Hawk], Sac, by Charles Bird King. Gulf States Paper Corporation.

Opposite: Top left, Wakechai [Crouching Eagle], Sac, by Charles Bird King. Gulf States Paper Corporation.■ Right, Peahmuska [The Fox Wending His Course], Fox, by Charles Bird King. Gulf States Paper Corporation.■ Bottom left, Wijunjon [The Light], Assiniboin, by Charles Bird King. Gulf States Paper Corporation. ■ Right, Timpoochee Barnard, Yuchi, by Charles Bird King. Gulf States Paper Corporation. ■ **Above:** Powasheek [To Dash the Water Off], Fox, by Charles Bird King. Gulf States Paper Corporation.

Nesouaquoit [Bear in the Fork of a Tree], Fox, by Charles Bird King. Sotheby Parke Bernet Inc., New York.

Notchimine [No Heart], Iowa, by Charles Bird King. National Collection of Fine Arts, Smithsonian Institution.

Keokuk, Sac, by Charles Bird King. Gulf States Paper Corporation.

Chenannoquot, Menominee, by
Charles Bird King.
Gulf States Paper Corporation.

Amiskquew [The Spoon], Menominee,
by Charles Bird King.
Gulf States Paper Corporation.

against the powerful Sioux. To blunt the full-scale war that threatened, the secretary of war invited the contending tribes to a general peace council in Washington that fall.

The Santee Sioux were the first to arrive, reaching the city in mid-September. Accompanied by their agent, Lawrence Taliaferro, the twenty-six chiefs and warriors created a mild sensation as they marched from the train station to Jimmy Maher's Globe Hotel at Fifteenth and Pennsylvania Avenue near the Treasury building. "They are fierce-looking, stout and able bodied men," noted a reporter from the *Washington National Intelligencer,* who observed their arrival from a safe distance. "Carrying about with them in the streets their bows and arrows, tomahawks, and pikes [they] appear to be a very warlike people. With due deference to 'the powers that be,' we doubt the propriety of these Indians being encouraged to walk about our streets armed 'cap-a-pie,' *without their attendants.*"[96]

No less imposing were the other delegations. The eighteen Yankton Sioux, Sac and Fox of the Missouri, and Iowa representatives arrived September 27. Hard on their heels came the Sac and Fox of the Mississippi. Although the reins of tribal authority had passed to Keokuk, the progressive leader who had refused to join the hostiles in their abortive uprising, Black Hawk and his son accompanied the delegation. They were not official delegates, however. According to the *Washington Globe,* the two warriors had wished "to visit the great towns and villages of their white brethren as free men having been taken through the country as prisoners."[97] Whatever his status, in any event, it was the romantic Black Hawk the public wished to see. As soon as word swept through the community that his party had arrived, the streets swelled with onlookers. The delegation did not disappoint its admirers. Marching proudly to the music of their drums and flutes, the thirty-four men, women, and children paraded up Pennsylvania Avenue to their quarters at the Virginia Coffee House, just a few doors away from the Globe Hotel.

Unfortunately, the vagaries of the weather, transportation, and mail service made coordinating arrivals of so many far-flung delegations impossible. As a result, the twenty-two Winnebagos who reached Washington on October 12 missed much of the congress. The twenty-five-member Pawnee, Omaha, Oto, and Missouri delegation fared even worse. These Indians did not arrive until mid-November, more than a week after the others had left the city.

No matter. By most standards the intertribal congress was a great success, although it did stretch the city's convention capabilities. Indeed, the only suitable place for holding the sessions proved to be the Reverend James Laurie's Presbyterian church on F Street, which the government rented for $400. A raised and carpeted platform, extending from the pulpit over the first few rows of pews, became the stage upon which the Indians and government officials conducted their business. Secretary of War Joel Poinsett usually presided over the sessions. He occupied center stage, flanked by an assortment of government bureaucrats and a continually changing cluster of dignitaries who included at times the vice president, secretary of the treasury, commissioner of Indian affairs, and ambassadors from several foreign countries. The Indians, grouped by tribe, sat on chairs in a semicircle facing Poinsett and the audience. The Sac and Fox were on the right, the Sioux on the left. In between were the Iowas and, when they finally arrived, the Winnebagos.

Keokuk, by George Catlin. National Collection of Fine Arts, Smithsonian Institution.

Keokuk, by George Catlin. National Collection of Fine Arts, Smithsonian Institution.

The sessions, which were held several times a week for more than a month, proved to be the highlight of the social season, attracting enormous crowds and receiving extensive press coverage. "An interesting talk took place between the Secretary of War and the Sioux chiefs, in Dr. Laurie's church yesterday. Keokuk also had his talk with the secretary," the *Intelligencer* informed its readers on October 6. Four days later, the newspaper reported that "a very numerous company of ladies and gentlemen arose at an early hour yesterday . . . to witness the interesting spectacle of an Indian council holding a talk, through their interpreters. All the seats in the church, both on the floor and in the galleries, were occupied, and many gentlemen remained standing in the aisles during the entire proceedings."

At times, the theatrical aspects of the affair distorted the true purpose of the congress. One churchgoer, disappointed at his inability to hear the deliberations, complained to the editor of the *Intelligencer*. "In common with the large audience present," he wrote, "I have had reason to regret that the Interpreters speak so low as to be utterly inaudible. Now, it would add greatly to the gratification of the public, whose wishes and accommodations have been provided for, if it should be made the duty of the interpreters to speak so loud as to be heard."[98]

Despite the hoopla and distractions, the congress, at least from the government's point of view, accomplished much. Five treaties were negotiated and signed in Washington; a sixth was signed by Iowa delegates before they reached home. The treaties, in theory, ironed out boundary disputes between the various tribes, thereby lessening opportunities for warfare. In reality, the treaties thinly disguised a land grab. Essentially, the Sioux and Winnebago delegates ceded all their holdings east of the Mississippi, including several islands they claimed in the river. The Sac and Fox sold more than a million acres of prime Iowa farm land.

These major cessions frightened the Iowas, who knew they would soon be pressured by their dispossessed yet powerful neighbors. In fact, the Iowa chief Notchimine tried to explain this to Poinsett. He presented a remarkably accurate map of the Mississippi River valley, drawn by one of his delegates, pointing out the territory his small and peaceful tribe had already lost to Sac and Fox encroachment. Keokuk, when Poinsett questioned him about this, responded: "It is true we have fought with the Iowas and taken a part of their land. If they want it back again, let them come and try to take it again."[99]

Keokuk's belligerence in this instance reflected the spirit of the entire council. Whatever its other accomplishments may have been, the congress did not bring peace to the Indian country. The tone of the meetings was firmly established when, at one of the early sessions, a Fox warrior taunted the Sioux delegation by waving a buffalo-horn headdress he had taken from a Santee corpse. When Poinsett tried to discuss a permanent peace between the two tribes, he failed completely.

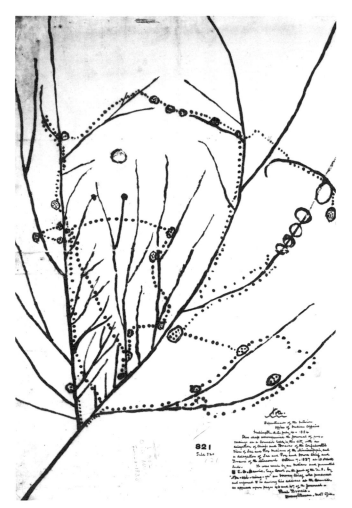

"My Father," an old Sioux chief told him, "you cannot make those people hear any good words, unless you drill their ears with sticks."

Another speaker agreed: "We have often made peace with them, but they would never observe any treaty. I would as soon think of making a treaty with that child," pointing to Keokuk's nine-year-old son, who sat on the floor between his legs, "as with a Sauk."

Such remarks could not go unanswered. Keokuk stepped forward and addressed Poinsett: "They tell you," he said, "that our ears must be bored with sticks; but, my Father, you could not penetrate their thick skulls in that way—it would require hot iron. They say they would as soon think of making peace with this child as with us—but they know better; for when they made war with us they found men."[100] If anything, the visiting tribesmen returned home with their hatred for each other intensified by their contact in Washington.

The delegates did not spend all their time in Dr. Laurie's church, of course. They made the typical jaunts to the White House, Capitol Hill, the Navy Yard, and the other attractions of the Great Father's city. Other outings were not so typical. One Friday afternoon, they visited the local racetrack where they attracted more attention than the horses. A few days later, the Sioux delegation demonstrated their war dance on the public square at Fourteenth Street. More than five thousand Washingtonians witnessed the well-advertised affair; thousands more never got close to the green because carriages, gigs, and vehicles of every description clogged streets for blocks around in violation of the regulations the police had made for the occasion. Black Hawk, Keokuk, and their entourage were on the field but refused to dance because of the boisterous and unruly crowd. Nevertheless, it was, according to the *Intelligencer,* "a very curious and exciting spectacle."[101]

Perhaps the most unusual episode of the intertribal congress occurred on Saturday evening, September 30, when the visiting tribesmen, except for the Sac and Fox who were still enroute to Washington, attended a ballet at the National Theater. Because the theater was crowded, the Indians were seated on the stage, where they almost outshone the ballerina, a Miss Nelson, in her role as the Mountain Sylph. The Indians paid no heed to the audience, for the dancer's grace and beauty held them spellbound; a crown of ostrich plumes flashed and fluttered as the Mountain Sylph darted lightly and swiftly across the stage. Suddenly, one of the Sioux warriors stood up and tossed his war bonnet of eagle feathers at Miss Nelson's feet. A second bonnet soon followed, and the ballerina stopped dancing. Tokacou, a celebrated Yankton chief, then stepped forward and handed the startled woman his splendid robe of white wolf skins. Not to be outdone, Moukaushka arose. This gallant young warrior would be dead within a month from one of the white man's dread diseases, but tonight his thoughts were only of the lovely Miss Nelson. He handed her his beautifully painted buffalo robe. He was offering this treasure, the interpreter explained to the audience, "to the beauty of Washington." The quick-thinking young woman acknowledged the gifts by plucking the ostrich plumes from her crown and giving one to each delegate. "The whole scene," the *Intelligencer* informed its readers, was "one of extraordinary and thrilling interest."[102]

The next day the Sioux delegation was seen striding along Pennsylvania Avenue toward the Capitol. Each warrior was proudly wearing a new military uniform, silver

epaulets, and hat. Tucked in each hatband was one of Miss Nelson's ostrich plumes.

Despite their crowded schedules, many of the delegates were able to sit long enough for King to capture them in oils. The artist was so busy, in fact, that he farmed out some of the work to George Cooke, his former pupil. According to an item in the *National Intelligencer* on September 29, 1837, however, King almost missed this important commission. The Sioux delegation, "under some superstitious impression," at first refused to sit for portraits. Thus, the editorial noted, "an excellent opportunity will be lost of adding to the valuable stock of Indian portraits now in the possession of the [War] Department."[103]

When the opportunistic George Catlin read the editorial, he promptly wrote to the commissioner of Indian affairs, Carey Harris, enclosing an advertisement for his exhibition of Indian paintings. There was nothing to worry about, Catlin said; he had already collected portraits "of the greater part of the chiefs & braves now in Washington," and "if the Indians now there refuse to sit for their likenesses . . . they will not be unchronicled to the World."[104]

This was not the first time that the enterprising artist had offered his services to the War Department. For several years Catlin had been following the fortunes of the Indian gallery, always with an eye to promoting his own interests. Five years earlier he had notified the department that he had portraits of Black Hawk and eight of his principal warriors, which he had painted during their imprisonment at Jefferson Barracks. "I had thoughts of sending them on to Washington & offer[ing] them to Government to add to their collection, but as that collection has been stopped . . . I suppose there is no prospect of their encouraging artists any further in making additions to it," he wrote in December 1832. At that time Catlin claimed to have portraits "of every Delegation of Indians which have been in Washington since that appropriation was stopped & could therefore make up the collection complete to the present time, on the plan that it was started, provided the Government should want them."[105]

The War Department had ignored Catlin in 1832 and it ignored him now. Instead, Commissioner Harris enlisted the aid of McKenney, who had been busily interviewing the Indian agents and delegates for his *History*. Surprisingly, even the persuasive McKenney had problems convincing the Indians to cooperate. "When you refer'd to me the business of having the Indians painted, I supposed that some additional celerity would follow —and that the ceremony of transferring to canvass, the likenesses of those selected for the artist would be soon over. But I was mistaken," he wrote Harris at the end of October. The Winnebago agent, Joseph Street, "has a large quantity of the snail in him, and, of course moves slowly," McKenney grumbled. [106] Further complicating the business was the reluctance of some of the principal warriors to sit for the artist. Black Hawk, for one, had refused. McKenney was not easily diverted from an objective, however, and before long the most important delegates, including the elusive Black Hawk, were safely on canvas.

A note from Lawrence Taliaferro, the Sioux agent, indicates just how touchy the matter of portraits was with the Indians. He sent Harris the names of six Indians and this terse statement: "The foregoing can be taken and not less without creating some unpleasant feeling."[107]

Apparently, few of the delegates left Washington unhappy because twenty-eight paintings were added to the War Department gallery. Cooke, who had opened a studio and gallery on Fourth Street and Pennsylvania Avenue only a few weeks before the delegations arrived, did nine—three Pawnees and six Sioux—for which he was paid thirty dollars each. A native of Maryland, Cooke had been a Georgetown merchant until the failure of his grocery and chinaware business in 1818. Turning to art for economic salvation, he traveled extensively both in the United States and abroad in the ensuing years, developing his skills as a portrait and landscape painter. Cooke never achieved the reputation of his mentor, but he was a skillful artist whom King could rely upon to do a creditable job.

King, for his nineteen portraits, received the princely sum of $730. These paintings are documented in two statements he submitted to the War Department for payment.[108] One, dated December 1837, lists the following portraits:

Black Hawk, "full length, size of life"	$ 60.00
Wa-pel-la, Fox chief	30.00
[illegible]	30.00
Wat-sha-ma-ne, Iowa chief	30.00
Tah-ko-ha, Iowa chief	30.00
A-she-au-kon, Sac chief	30.00
Pa-naw-sr, Sac chief, "extra"	40.00
Nin-she-o-shuck, Sac chief	30.00
"name unknown—Taliaferro party"	30.00
A-mon-ni, Yankton Sioux	30.00
Ke-o-kuck & son, Mee-sair-want	150.00
Not-cha-mon-ni, Iowa	30.00
	$520.00

In February 1838 King submitted the following statement:

Shi-he-gash-waw-shushe, Omawhaw	$ 30.00
La-ke-too-nee-ra-sha, Pawnee	30.00
We-ke-roo-tan, Ottoe	30.00
Yaw-che-ke-sug-ga, Missouri	30.00
No-way-ke-sug-ga, Ottoe	30.00
Le-shaw-loo-pa-le-hoo, Pawnee Loup	30.00
Waw-ro-na-sah, Ottoe	30.00
	$210.00

The portrait of Keokuk and his son at $150 was the most expensive painting King ever did for the government.

Isaac Cooper, still in business in 1837, framed all the portraits. For Keokuk and his son he charged the War Department $10, for Black Hawk, $8. Two others were $6 each, the rest $2.50.

McKenney, no doubt a constant visitor at King's studio, wasted little time in requisitioning the portraits for his own use. On October 30 he asked Commissioner Harris "to cause *all* the portraits that have been taken, put up in a box, and directed to Edwd. C. Biddle Esqr. Minor Street Philad. and sent by the Rail road line. Whatever expense may attend on the box, & the packing, & postage, will [be] pd. by Mr. Biddle, as also the expense of sending them back. King, & Cooke, had the work. Let *both* be applied to, for the result of their labors." McKenney assured Harris that the portraits would be "put immediately in the hand of the Lithographist, so as to have them back to you with the least possible delay."[109]

Other portraits went to Philadelphia as they were completed. At the end of December, King himself asked Harris for permission to send Biddle the portraits of Moukaushka and Tokacou. Biddle returned four of the paintings a month later with the promise that the others would "follow soon."[110] In the meantime, he needed the painting of Keokuk and his son. Would Harris permit King to send it to him?

Despite all the assurances, most of the portraits were not promptly returned. In fact, they remained in Philadelphia so long that a worried King personally wrote Biddle a letter of enquiry. The publisher blamed the delay on "the Artist in Colouring his patterns" and promised to return them all within a week. "I regret," Biddle wrote July 7, when he shipped the five remaining portraits to the Indian office, "that I was obliged to retain them so long & beg of you to accept my sincere thanks for the loan of *them* & for the assistance rendered me in the prosecution of the book itself."[111]

Five years passed before King again received a commission from the War Department. This time his subjects were leaders of two relatively obscure tribes the federal government wanted to impress with a special honor. One was Joseph Polis, a Penobscot Indian from Maine; the other was John Quinney, chief of the Stockbridges, an Algonquin tribe then living near Green Bay, Wisconsin.

The Penobscots were not numerous. At most, a few hundred mixed-blood survivors of this once important colonial tribe eked out a meager existence in central Maine near Bangor. The government had ignored the Penobscots in the removal program and had never assigned an agent to the tribe. Perhaps Polis was in Washington in the spring of 1842 attempting to restore some of the luster his people had once enjoyed as members of the powerful Abnaki Confederacy, which had welcomed the first white men to their shore some three centuries earlier. His mission was somewhat successful for he had an audience with the Great Father, who directed the commissioner of Indian affairs to give him peace medals for the tribe's first and second chiefs. The medals, the commissioner informed the Penobscot chiefs in his accompanying letter, were "a mark of the [president's] . . . friendly feeling for you and your people." The commission to King for Polis's portrait was another mark of that esteem. As Crawford explained, the Great Father "was glad to see Joseph Porus [Polis] at Washington, and I will direct his face to be painted and kept that we may remember him. When we look at him we will know we are looking at a friend"[112]

The Stockbridges, like the Penobscots, cast only a shadow of their former importance. In Massachusetts, as members of the Mahican Confederacy, they had been allies of the British in the colonial wars with the French and Americans, wars that left the Stockbridges homeless and decimated by 1785. The 200 survivors at first lived with their Oneida friends in New York, and then the government removed both tribes to Green Bay, where they shared a reservation with the Munsees, a tribal remnant of the Delawares. By the middle of the nineteenth century, the Stockbridges were a dispirited and embittered people.

Unable to get satisfaction from local authorities for various grievances against the federal government, the tribe in November 1841 sent Quinney and John W. Chicks, another chief, to Washington. The two ambassadors carried a letter of introduction from James D. Doty, governor of Wisconsin and ex officio superintendent of Indian affairs, who wrote: "I have long known . . . [them] as chiefs of this Tribe, and I have always regarded them as the most respectable men in it. They are regarded by the Tribe as its chiefs and ought to be received as such in preference to those who have not heretofore been so considered."[113]

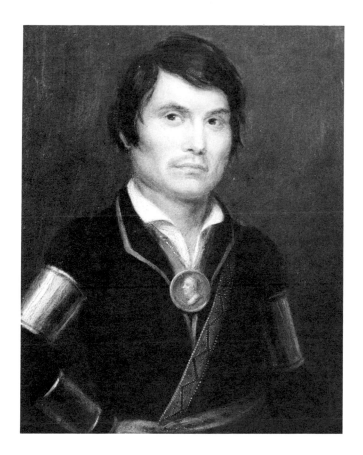 

Quinney and Chicks were in Washington more than six months. During that time they submitted several petitions to Congress, which were settled to varying degrees of satisfaction. One particularly troublesome grievance concerned an annual annuity payment of $350 promised the Stockbridges *"forever"* when they signed the treaty of 1794 between the United States and the Six Nations of the Iroquois Confederacy. The tribe had received this money each year until 1838; then the government abruptly terminated the annuity, claiming the Stockbridges were not entitled to it. Tribal leaders at first had accepted the decision, but, Quinney and Chicks informed President John Tyler, "in looking at the treaty, which we found on the 50th page of the Book of treaties, it says that . . . [the annuity] shall be paid yearly, *forever*. We therefore appeal to our Great Father, that justice may be done us, that the amount now due may be paid us, & that in future we may receive the amount yearly, which was so long paid us."[114]

In this instance, the delegates got their way. The commissioner of Indian affairs had stopped the payments upon discovering that only two Stockbridge families, not representatives of the entire tribe, had signed the 1794 treaty. Because of that technicality the commissioner felt the agreement was not legally binding. Perhaps not, but the sum involved was very small; to avoid further hard feelings on the part of the Stockbridges, the commissioner authorized resumption of the payments. Unfortunately, other claims were not so easily resolved. One dispute, over money due the tribe for the sale of land in Wisconsin to the federal government, remained unsettled until the turn of the century.

Nevertheless, Quinney and Chicks represented their tribes well while in Washington. They conducted their affairs with dignity and they deserved special recognition. Chicks received a peace medal, but that would not be enough for so acculturated and educated an Indian as Quinney. Why not have his portrait painted? someone suggested. The commissioner of Indian affairs in May 1842 sent Quinney and Polis, who was concluding his business in Washington at the same time, to visit King and arrange for sittings.

The double commission probably surprised King. The new editors of the *History of the Indian Tribes of North America* already had more than enough portraits to bring that mammoth project to a successful close, and interest in the War Department gallery had waned in recent years. Indeed, the portraits of Polis and Quinney were not even added to the gallery because Secretary of War John Bell only a few months earlier had donated the paintings and McKenney's "curiosities" to the newly formed National Institute.

Washingtonians enjoying the delightful May weather paid scant heed to the artist as they strolled past his shaded yard. On fine days King usually set up his easel outside, and the fashionably dressed Quinney attracted little notice. What a change from the days when crowds would gather to watch King working on a portrait of a painted warrior garbed in his finest regalia. In twenty years an entire generation of Indian leaders had passed before his easel—Petalesharro, Pushmataha, Red Jacket, Keokuk, Black Hawk, and now Quinney. Did King suspect this portrait would be the last in that marvelous series? How appropriate that it was of an acculturated Indian. The wild warrior would inevitably vanish, McKenney had often predicted when justifying the portrait gallery. At one time King may have found that difficult to believe. The artist's own father, Captain Zebulon King, had died at Indian hands. Now, however, instead of resolving their grievances with the tomahawk and scalping knife, Indian leaders were just as wont to ask their congressmen to iron out the difficulties. The white-haired painter recorded that transition with an appropriate flourish. He sketched John Quinney holding a rolled sheet of paper that reads: "Memorial to Congress, 1842."

The portraits of Polis and Quinney are not representative of King's better work. They seem hurriedly, even carelessly done. The bodies are ill-proportioned; the arms and hands, especially, are poorly modeled. Were the Indians restless and anxious to be on their way? Did King consider the commission unworthy of his best effort? His fee for the portraits was only forty-six dollars, including frames, scarcely more than it had been when, twenty years earlier to the month, he had done the portraits of the O'Fallon delegation.

VI

The Fate of the Portraits

By the time King completed the portraits of Polis and Quinney, his fame had spread far beyond the Washington community, thanks to the wide publicity given the magnificent McKenney and Hall lithographs. King, of course, already enjoyed a comfortable existence and social prominence, but the acclaim accorded the *History of the Indian Tribes of North America* ensured him a steady flow of commissions. Just as King's reputation grew, interest in the gallery also revived.

Indeed, the War Department gallery was highly coveted by the National Institute, a private association originally founded in Washington in 1818 as the Columbian Institute for the Promotion of Art and Science. Drawing its membership primarily from army and naval officers, diplomats, and "professional gentlemen" employed by the federal government, the institute maintained a cabinet of curiosities and a library and sponsored lectures on science and philosophy. In 1840, hoping to become the beneficiary of the strange and wonderful bequest of James Smithson, the British nobleman who left $500,000 to the United States "to found at Washington an establishment . . . for the increase and diffusion of knowledge among men," the Columbian Institute changed its name and constitution and broadened its scope. The institute's future seemed assured when, two years later, Congress made it the official curator of all collections in the arts and sciences in the custody of the federal government and allowed it to house the material in the recently completed Patent Office building at Eighth and G streets in Washington, D.C.

Several months before the institute received official confirmation of its curatorial responsibilities, a three-member committee began visiting government departments in search of collections. One of the first stops was the War Department building where the committee interviewed newly appointed Secretary of War John Bell. "Would you be willing to donate the Indian portraits and curiosities to the National Institute?" they asked. Bell, probably delighted at the prospect of eliminating the clutter from the crowded quarters of the Bureau of Indian Affairs, readily agreed, and McKenney's once cherished archives was transferred within the week. The overjoyed officers of the National Institute promptly passed a resolution which at once thanked Bell for his generosity and asked another favor: "We have the honor of requesting for the Institution, one of the copies in the War Department, of the Lythographic prints and historical sketches, having reference to these Portraits." Bell agreed that the "prints and sketches" were "properly appendages" to the portraits, so the institute also received one of the fifty sets of the McKenney and Hall volumes the War Department had purchased.[115]

The officers of the institute wasted no time before displaying their new accession; in less than a week the paintings were hung and the curiosities were safely behind glass in the exhibit hall. One of the first to describe the archives in its new setting was David

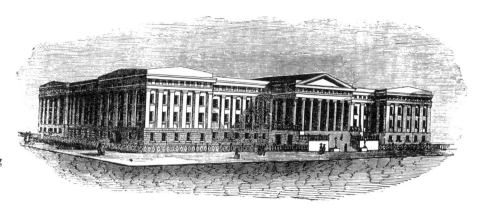

Patent Office building, from engraving
in the National Institute catalog.
Smithsonian Institution Archives.

Cooke, a merchant from Philadelphia. "The museum is in the Story above [the Patent Office] in one large room the whole width and breadth of the building," he informed his wife on June 20, 1842. "Indian implements and curiosities [are] on one side of the room—the other side is similar to the Philadelphia museum—[and] 150 likenesses of Indian warriors are hung around the room."[116]

Despite this auspicious beginning, the National Institute failed to receive the Smithson bequest. Instead, Congress in 1846 chose to establish the Smithsonian Institution, which rapidly became the nation's center for the arts and sciences. The National Institute tried to compete but could not survive without federal financial support and finally collapsed after almost two decades of struggle. Its collections, untended and disordered, remained in the Patent Office building to the end. Even during the institute's better days, however, the material evidently received only minimal curatorial care. An exhibit catalog of 1855 complained that the Indian paintings were "placed too high up to discern the features closely," while only a few of the more prominent subjects, such as Red Jacket and Keokuk, were even identified.[117]

The paintings were temporarily rescued from oblivion in 1858 when the National Institute formally disbanded and transferred its more important specimens to the Smithsonian Institution. Joseph Henry, the first secretary of the Smithsonian, placed the portraits in a second-floor gallery where another fine collection of American Indian portraits and scenes, by the New York artist John Mix Stanley, was already on display. The combined exhibit, according to Henry, formed "the most valuable collection in existence of illustrations of the features, costumes, and habits of the aborigines of this country."[118]

The Stanley collection probably rivaled the War Department gallery in scope and importance. Like Catlin before him, Stanley had been attracted by American Indian life and for ten years traveled extensively in the Far West. He visited forty-three tribes and painted 154 portraits and scenes of everyday life before returning to the East in 1851. He loaned his collection, which he valued at $19,000, to the Smithsonian, hoping that either the institution or Congress would purchase his paintings as the nucleus of a national gallery of art.

Several times over the next decade he petitioned both houses of Congress and the Smithsonian board of regents to buy his collection. With the petitions, he enclosed numerous endorsements, including one from McKenney, then in retirement in New York City. Age had dimmed neither McKenney's verbosity nor his fervor for the Native Americans. "You know," he wrote, "I have seen the Indians in their forest homes, and under every phase of their character. Stanley has immortalized himself by the reflex he has given of this down trodden race." Nothing could be more lifelike, McKenney thought. "The costume is perfect—It is all a reality—truth is the foundation of all." In fact, he continued, "I consider it the last best offering of this sort which will ever come to us from the wilderness home of this people. Their destiny as a race is sealed. They will soon be lost to our sight forever."[119]

Stanley's petitions did arouse some congressional support. The Senate Committee on Indian Affairs in 1853 went so far as to refer one of the petitions to Luke Lea, commissioner of Indian affairs, for his views as to "the value, quality and truthfulness of the paintings." The commissioner's reply is touched with irony. Scarcely a decade had passed since King's paintings had been transferred to the National Institute, yet evidently no memory of them lingered at the Bureau of Indian Affairs. "As the aboriginal inhabitants of our country are fast disappearing from the face of the Earth," Lea replied, "there seems to be an increasing regret that the Government has not taken more timely and efficient measures for preserving memorials of the race. A National Portrait Gallery of distinguished Indians, permanently located at the seat of Government, would certainly be an object of general interest and that interest would continue to increase with the lapse of time." Echoing McKenney's pleas of a quarter of a century earlier, Lea urged the committee to provide a small sum annually that the bureau could use to commission portraits of prominent Indian visitors to Washington. "Before long," he assured the Senate committee, "a valuable collection could be made that would be highly creditable to the Government."[120]

Joseph Henry also wished to expand the gallery of Indian portraits, but he had a novel suggestion for reducing the cost: he recommended in 1858 that prominent Indian leaders be photographed instead of sitting for expensive and time-consuming oil portraits. In either case, he thought the combined gallery must be kept together for posterity, and he urged Congress to purchase the Stanley paintings, "which will become more and more valuable in the progress of the gradual extinction of the race of which they are such faithful representations."[121]

Despite such glowing testimonials, Stanley failed to convince Congress of the need for a national gallery of art. His efforts to sell the collection to the government were equally fruitless. The artist, however, never lost hope that a benefactor would intercede, and so kept his paintings on display at the Smithsonian for more than a decade. No doubt the addition of the King portraits to the Smithsonian collections buoyed Stanley's belief that the creation of a national art gallery was inevitable.

The many Indian delegations that continued to trek to Washington each year certainly appreciated the paintings. Where once a proud McKenney had ushered the bewildered visitors into his office for a glimpse of his prized gallery, government officials now made a stop at the Smithsonian mandatory for each delegation. The King and Stanley paintings seldom failed to make a favorable impression. "They examined with great interest the various portraits of Indians, and sketches of Indian life, as hunting, [and] dancing," wrote a Smithsonian clerk about one such delegation. Although they were disappointed at finding no portraits or scenes from their tribe, a Stanley painting of warriors dancing around a captive white woman and her child fascinated them. "They gathered in groups in front of it and made many remarks about it in their own language."[122]

Thanks to the diligence of William J. Rhees, chief clerk of the Smithsonian, there is a fairly complete catalog of the War Department gallery in the *Guide to the*

Petalesharro the Younger, son of the Petalesharro immortalized by Charles Bird King, attributed to A. Zeno Shindler, who photographed several Indians during their visit to Washington in January 1858. Perhaps it was this series of photographs that prompted Joseph Henry to suggest continuing the Indian gallery with the camera instead of the paintbrush. National Anthropological Archives, Smithsonian Institution.

Below, west range of the Smithsonian in 1862. Several Indian portraits can be seen on display. Smithsonian Institution Archives. ■ Bottom, only known photograph of the King and Stanley gallery, taken sometime before the Smithsonian fire of 1865. National Anthropological Archives, Smithsonian Institution.

Heavily retouched photograph of the Smithsonian building, taken during the fire of January 24, 1865. Smithsonian Institution Archives.

Smithsonian Institution which he published in 1859 (see page 143). Where possible, Rhees provided the Indian and English names for each subject, the year the portrait was painted, and the name of the artist. A few of the portraits appear simply as numbers because neither the name nor tribe could be determined. Although invaluable, the catalog must be used with caution. Many of the names as well as the attributions are inaccurate. Of the 147 paintings, Rhees attributes only sixty-one original portraits to King, plus another twenty-five the artist copied from James Otto Lewis. From attributions McKenney provided in his *History of the Indian Tribes of North America* and from government financial records, however, ninety-nine portraits in the Rhees list are known to be by King. Doubtless, most of the unattributed portraits are his work as well. When copies given to the delegates, replicas, and portraits not part of the original gallery are included, the total number of King's Indian portraits approaches two hundred.

Although the integrity and security of the King portraits now seemed assured, in fact they survived only until the afternoon of January 24, 1865, when fire consumed the entire gallery. To keep warm in an unusually cold winter, a crew of workmen renovating the second-floor exhibit hall had set up a stove, connecting the stovepipe to a chimney they found in a closet. Eight days later the ceiling burst into flame; within minutes the room and its contents were destroyed. The entire wing suffered damage, but fireproof walls saved the building from complete ruin. An investigation later revealed that the stovepipe had not been connected to a chimney but to a ventilator shaft that opened onto wooden beams under the slate roof.

The loss was tragic and terrible. All but a few of the King and Stanley paintings were destroyed. The fire left Stanley anguished and financially broken, for he never received a penny in compensation. Destiny was kinder to King. The artist never knew the fate of his gallery because he had died three years earlier, just a few months short of his seventy-seventh birthday.

VII

Charles Bird King's Artistic Legacy

Despite the Smithsonian fire, a number of King's American Indian portraits can be found today in public and private collections both in the United States and abroad. Most of these paintings are replicas, although there are a few original oil portraits. In addition, a member of the King family owns an exquisite set of sixteen charcoal sketches that may have served as models for his Indian subjects. Of the known oil portraits, five are in the custody of the Smithsonian Institution, five are in the White House, nine in the Danish National Museum in Copenhagen, six in the Thomas Gilcrease Institute of American History and Art in Tulsa, Oklahoma, and seventeen in the art collection of the Gulf States Paper Corporation in Tuscaloosa, Alabama.

The history of the five White House portraits is especially interesting: Eagle of Delight, Shaumonekusse, Petalesharro, Monchousia, and Sharitarish were members of the 1821 O'Fallon delegation—and the most popular of King's Indian subjects.

The original owner of the White House paintings was Patrick Macaulay of Baltimore. In 1826 he sent them to his friend Christopher Hughes, then chargé d'affaires to the Court of the Netherlands, along with the names and descriptions of the subjects and the circumstances of their visit to Washington. "I do not know whether you take the same interest in these people that I do," Macaulay wrote, "but I commit the Redskins wholly to your charge to do with as you think fit."[123]

The five portraits remained abroad for more than a century, and were not returned to the United States until 1962 when the employees of Sears, Roebuck and Company purchased and presented them to Mrs. John F. Kennedy. The portraits now hang in the White House library where all Americans can see them and, as Sharitarish once hoped, "reflect on the times that are past."

The story behind the Danish collection is equally intriguing. The museum purchased the portraits at auction in 1854 from the estate of Peter von Scholton, who was governor-general of the Danish West Indies from 1827 to 1848. Von Scholton received the portraits from President Andrew Jackson in 1830 when he was serving as envoy extraordinary to the United States for the Danish government. Despite the absence of documentation for this transaction, the gift seems likely. The Danish historian Kaj Birket-Smith, who wrote a brief history of the paintings, certainly accepts this explanation. "How else," Birket-Smith asks, "could Von Scholton have come into possession of as many as nine pictures by an American artist, who had no great fame out of his own country?" At the time of his death the governor also had a framed lithograph of President Jackson among his personal effects, a fact that strengthens this conclusion in the historian's mind. "There were certainly so few points of contact between the extremely aristocratic Scholton and the rather ill-bred and ruthless Jackson that the presence of a portrait like the above mentioned can only indicate a personal connection between them," he writes.[124]

CHARLES BIRD KING.

Born in Newport A.D. 1785. Died in Washington, D.C. 1862.

This Portrait painted by himself when 70 years of age.

Attributing much of his success in life to an early taste for Literature and Art, cultivated within the walls of this Library, he repaid the obligation by successive Donations to this Institution. At his death he made to it the munificent Bequest of Real Estate yielding Nine Thousand Dollars, his Library, his valuable Engravings, and more than Two Hundred Paintings which adorn these walls. A life-long Friend, —— May his Name and Benefactions be held in perpetual remembrance.

American records are silent on the subject of these King paintings, but they do confirm that Von Scholton visited Jackson in October 1830 in an unsuccessful effort to arrange advantageous terms of commerce for the Danish West-Indian Islands, which today are known as the Virgin Islands. Jackson, in fact, arranged passage for Von Scholton's return to St. Croix aboard the United States sloop of war *Vincennes.*

The Danish collection includes two unique portraits—those of Young Cornplanter, a Seneca chief, and Choncape, an Oto chief who was a member of the O'Fallon delegation. The painting of Young Cornplanter may be an original portrait, because it was not in the War Department gallery and it was not included in McKenney and Hall's *History of the Indian Tribes of North America.* On the back of this painting, King wrote: "Young Corn Planter, Senecas Indian, New York, Aid to Red Jacket. Original Portrait by C. B. King 1827. He is a half breed." Red Jacket visited McKenney that year to protest his removal from office by the Seneca tribal council. Presumably Young Cornplanter accompanied the aged warrior on this visit as he did in March 1823, when the following item appeared in the *Washington National Intelligencer:* "Red Jacket and Young Cornplanter, . . . Seneca chiefs, arrived in Washington on official business on Tuesday evening."[125] The portrait of Choncape, although it is the only copy known to be extant, was in the War Department gallery and was copied lithographically.

Von Scholton was not the only European to obtain Indian portraits. In July 1826 King borrowed the "head of Keo-Kuck, Fox Chief," from the War Department because "Count Gramasy wishes to take a copy to France."[126] Presumably other Indian portraits found their way to the Continent in this way.

The other major collection that deserves mention is the one King gave to the Redwood Library and Athenaeum in his native Newport. Although the artist had left Rhode Island as a teen-ager and lived in the District of Columbia until his death, he always considered Newport his home. For years he summered in Newport, where he maintained a residence and studio. This enduring sentiment baffled even King. "I sometimes think it strange that I should have so great an attachment to Newport and its people by whom I have been so much neglected," the artist complained just three years before his death. "When I commenced painting, the extent of my patronage [there] was $200. Since then I have only had a Forty dollar head, except from my relations. [Only] once in my life was I invited out to dinner, and in my last visit I was not asked into any house but those of two New York cottagers."[127] Nevertheless, King contributed greatly to the welfare of the community. Always fond of children, he liked to visit Newport's schools and often purchased supplies and equipment the city fathers could not afford.

He was especially generous to the Redwood Library, incorporated in 1747 and located in the oldest library structure in the United States still used for its original purpose. As early as 1829 he gave the library copies of his portraits of Shaumonekusse and Eagle of Delight, which had been on exhibition at the Boston Athenaeum. The agent for the art show was instructed to forward the portraits to the Redwood Library "as a present from me," King informed the board of directors. From time to time thereafter, he contributed money, books, and works of art. "This day I have sent the fifth box containing 15 pictures, making seventy in all," King wrote on May 24, 1859. "While I continue my exhibition here

King occasionally did more than one view of a particularly interesting or important subject such as the Fox chief Nesouaquoit. This version was part of the War Department gallery and was reproduced in McKenney and Hall's *History of the Indian Tribes of North America*. King also did a full figure of Nesouaquoit (color plate on page 97) that went to the Redwood Library. Chicago Historical Society.

[in Washington] I must retain the most attractive of my own paintings. I have sent you several to help the nakedness of your walls for the present. At my death you will have the best of *my own paintings*."[128] True to his word, King left the Redwood his personal library, several volumes of bound engravings, a large sum of money, and seventy-five paintings. In all, the Redwood Library received 212 paintings from King, of which twenty-one were Indian portraits.

The importance of the Redwood collection cannot be overstated. Not only was it the largest group of Indian portraits outside the War Department gallery, but it constituted King's finest work. According to George G. King, his executor, the paintings selected for the Redwood Library were "the best" of his collection "as it was Mr. King's wish that they should be."[129] The Indian portraits are indeed superb; generally, they are superior to replicas found elsewhere and may have served as models for them. A few, such as the paintings of The Light and Chenannoquot, are unique. They were neither in the War Department gallery nor reproduced in McKenney and Hall. Others, including Powasheek, Keokuk, Wabaunsee, Pushmataha, Wanata, Black Hawk, and Nesouaquoit, differ from the lithographs in pose or attire.

Although the Redwood Library still has custody of many of King's paintings, the trustees of the financially hardpressed institution in 1970 auctioned the Indian portraits. Most were sold to museums or art galleries, but a few slipped into private hands, at least one going to an overseas buyer. Fortunately, the impact of this regrettable dispersion was softened by the resolution of Jack Warner, president of Gulf States Paper Corporation, to purchase as many of the King portraits as possible and keep them together in one collection.

Gulf States first became aware of Charles Bird King's Indian portraits through the McKenney and Hall lithographic copies; in 1969 the company used reproductions of these lithographs in an advertising campaign. Searching for background information, the staff wrote to the Redwood Library. The reply contained an almost parenthetical comment that the library planned to sell the collection through Parke Bernet in New York. On a whim, the sales department head asked Parke Bernet for details of the impending sale, then took the catalog to Warner, thinking he might add to the company's art collection the portrait of Pushmataha, a Choctaw leader whose domain included areas where Gulf States now manages forest land.

Warner's enthusiasm far exceeded the acquisition of one portrait. He attended the sale in New York and bought ten of the twenty-one paintings. The Indian portraits quickly became one of the main attractions at the company's corporate headquarters.

Meanwhile, the Gulf States collection of King Indian portraits has continued to grow. The first ten from the Parke Bernet auction were soon joined by four more from the Redwood group that had originally been sold to other buyers. A fifteenth portrait—that of The Good Martin—was acquired from the University of Pennsylvania Museum in Philadelphia. And early in 1975 two portraits previously unknown to students of King's works were sold by the King family. These fine portraits of Keokuk and Petalesharro were added to the Gulf States collection, bringing the present total to seventeen.

The story of the King portraits would be incomplete without mention of the charcoal sketches, only recently discovered by the present owners, Mr. and Mrs. Bayard LeRoy King of Saunderstown, Rhode Island. The sketches had long remained unknown in a file cabinet of family papers assembled by George Gordon King over a period of years before the First World War. Charles Bird King and the grandfather of George Gordon King were first cousins. After the death of George Gordon King in 1922, the present owner's father, a nephew, inherited the file cabinet, but apparently never knew of the existence of the drawings, as he never mentioned them to his son. When his father died, Bayard King in turn inherited the family papers in 1963. It was not until eleven years later, when living in Caroline County, Virginia, that he began sifting through the material and discovered the unique original drawings in an envelope labeled "Charles Bird King." In addition to sixteen Indian sketches, there is one of the Marquis de Lafayette that King did from life in 1825 when the French hero of the American Revolution visited Washington, D.C.

The sketches add an exciting new dimension to our knowledge of King as an artist. Drawn on rough, gray paper, the sketches are approximately the same size—6½ by 9½ inches. The modeling is done with a sure, deft hand. Indeed, the crisp sketches seem to have more vitality than some of the paintings themselves. All but two of the sketches can be matched either to existing portraits or to lithographs in McKenney and Hall. The poses are identical. It appears, in fact, that King used them to trace the outlines for his replicas, because the back of each sketch is blackened from many rubbings and the faint indentations of a stylus are visible on several of the faces. It is a technique other portraitists of his day employed. Whatever their purpose, the sketches are an integral part of the story, and fortunately they surfaced in time for inclusion in this book.

Only in recent years has Charles Bird King begun to receive the attention he richly deserves. He was a good if not greatly gifted artist, whose oeuvre included a wide range of subjects; his Indian portraits have assured him a permanent niche in the artistic heritage of the United States. Were it not for this gentle artist from Rhode Island, who never even went west of the Mississippi, the pictorial record of the Native Americans in the early years of the Republic would be meager indeed. Even his contemporaries recognized this fact. "He painted with a very considerable degree of vigor, had an eye for color, and many of his most hasty productions are his best, for he has caught the spirit of the subject," wrote the unknown author of King's obituary in the *Newport Mercury*. "This is particularly true in regard to the large number of portraits of Indians who visited Washington from time to time during the artist's life, who were painted by him in their war paint and wild costumes, thus preserving the characteristics of a race that has nearly disappeared and will be lost sight of forever." [130]

Top: Left, finished portrait of Rantchewaime [Female Flying Pigeon], Iowa. Gulf States Paper Corporation. (Color plate of Rantchewaime painting is on page 62.) ■ Right, charcoal sketch of Rantchewaime. ■ **Bottom:** Left, finished portrait of Moanahonga [Great Walker], Iowa. Thomas Gilcrease Institute of American History and Art. (Color plate of Moanahonga is on page 61.) ■ Right, charcoal sketch of Moanahonga. Sketches courtesy of Bayard LeRoy King.

Mak·we·hah·mak, Goway Chief.
(Great Walker.)

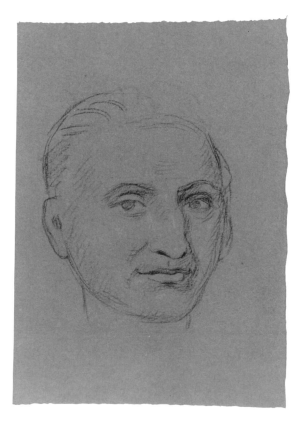

Top: Left, finished portrait of Peahmuska [The Fox Wending His Course], Fox, Gulf States Paper Corporation. (Color plate of Peahmuska painting is on page 94.) ■ Right, charcoal sketch of Peahmuska. ■ **Bottom:** Left, Keesheswa [The Sun], Fox, charcoal sketch. ■ Right, Unknown, charcoal sketch. Sketches courtesy of Bayard LeRoy King.

127

Top: Left, Wakechai, Sac, charcoal sketch. (Color plate of Wakechai painting is on page 94.) ■ Right, No-Tin [Wind], Chippewa, charcoal sketch. ■ **Bottom:** Left, Taiomah [The Bear Whose Screams Make Rocks Tremble], Fox, charcoal sketch. ■ Right, Peechekir [Buffalo], Chippewa, charcoal sketch. Sketches courtesy of Bayard LeRoy King.

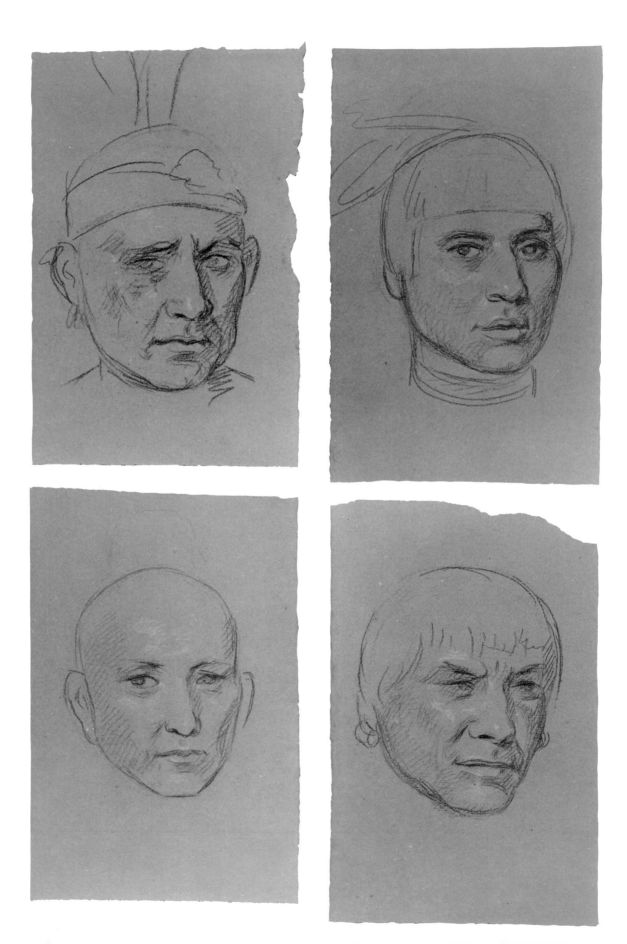

Top: Left, Kaipolequa [White-nosed Fox], Fox, charcoal sketch. ■ Right, Pashepahaw [Stabber], Sac, charcoal sketch. ■ **Bottom:** Left, Tahcolaquoit, Sac, charcoal sketch. ■ Right, Eshtahumbah [Sleepy Eyes], Sioux, charcoal sketch. Sketches courtesy of Bayard LeRoy King.

Left, Amiskquew, Menominee, charcoal sketch. (Color plate of Amiskquew painting is on page 100.) ■ Right, Unknown, charcoal sketch. Sketches courtesy of Bayard LeRoy King.

Notes

Abbreviations for sources:

IA LR Office of Indian Affairs, Letters Received, Record Group 75, National Archives

IA LS Office of Indian Affairs, Letters Sent, Record Group 75, National Archives

IT LS Office of Indian Trade, Letters Sent, Record Group 75, National Archives

SW LR Office of the Secretary of War, Letters Received, Record Group 107, National Archives

SW LS Office of the Secretary of War, Letters Sent, Record Group 107, National Archives

1. Thomas L. McKenney to Jared Sparks, April 20, 1833, Jared Sparks Papers (Houghton Library, Harvard University).

2. The best published sources on the life and career of Charles Bird King are John C. Ewers, "Charles Bird King, Painter of Indian Visitors to the Nation's Capital," *Annual Report of the Board of Regents of the Smithsonian Institution . . . 1953* (Washington, D.C., 1954), pp. 463-74; and Andrew F. Cosentino, "Charles Bird King: An Appreciation," *American Art Journal* VI (May 1974): 54-71.

3. Papers relating to Zebulon and Charles Bird King in the custody of Bayard LeRoy King, Saunderstown, R.I.

4. Quotes by Louisa and John Quincy Adams are from Cosentino, "Charles Bird King: An Appreciation," p. 67.

5. Thomas Donaldson, *The George Catlin Indian Gallery in the U.S. National Museum (Smithsonian Institution) with a Memoir and Statistics* (Washington, D.C., 1887), p. 795.

6. For a comprehensive survey of McKenney's career, see Herman J. Viola, *Thomas L. McKenney, Architect of America's Early Indian Policy* (Chicago, 1974).

7. McKenney to T. Lewis, Nov. 22, 1820, IT LS, vol. F, p. 81; Thomas L. McKenney, *Sketches of a Tour to the Lakes, of the Character and Customs of the Chippeway Indians, and of Incidents Connected with the Treaty of Fond Du Lac* (Baltimore, 1827), p. 320.

8. McKenney to Factors, July 22, 1817, IT LS, vol. D, pp. 376-77.

9. McKenney to John W. Johnson, Aug. 26, 1820, *ibid.,* vol. F, p. 38.

10. Second Auditor's Accounts (first series), Nos. 5724, 8062, 8100, 8668, 9445, 9955, 10163, 10584, 11679, 12910, 12923, 15437; (second series), Nos. 1154, 1421, 7071, Records of the General Accounting Office, RG 217, Washington National Records Center, Suitland, Md. (henceforth WNRC).

11. McKenney to James Barbour, April 7, 1825, IA LS, vol. 1, p. 441.

12. Benjamin O'Fallon to John C. Calhoun, April 5, 1821, SW LR.

13. O'Fallon to Calhoun, Sept. 25, 1819, printed in Clarence E. Carter, ed., *The Territorial Papers of the United States* (Washington, D.C.), XV: 563.

14. O'Fallon to William Clark, May 10, 1817, *ibid.*, pp. 264-65.

15. Benjamin Perley Poore, *Perley's Reminiscences* (Philadelphia, 1886), I: 42-44.

16. Quoted in Thomas L. McKenney and James Hall, *The Indian Tribes of North America, with Biographical Sketches and Anecdotes of the Principal Chiefs,* ed. by Frederick Webb Hodge (Edinburgh, 1933), I: 163, fn 9.

17. The most authoritative work on peace medals is Francis Paul Prucha, *Indian Peace Medals in American History* (Madison, 1971).

18. *Washington National Intelligencer,* Feb. 11, 1822.

19. *Washington Gazette,* Feb. 13, 1822.

20. *Washington National Intelligencer,* Feb. 16, 1822.

21. *Ibid.,* Feb. 11, 1822.

22. *Ibid.,* Feb. 16, 1822.

23. Patrick Macaulay to Christopher Hughes, Oct. 2, 1826, printed in *Penrith* [England] *Observer,* Dec. 30, 1924.

24. *Washington Gazette,* Jan. 2, 1822.

25. *Philadelphia Franklin Gazette,* Feb. 11, 1822; *Washington National Intelligencer,* March 7, 1822; William Faux, *Memorable Days in America* (London, 1823), reprinted in Reuben Gold Thwaites, ed., *Early Western Travels, 1748-1846,* XII: 51.

26. Faux, *Memorable Days in America,* p. 52.

27. Quoted in Hodge, *Indian Tribes of North America,* I: 216, fn 10.

28. Laura Wirt to Louisa Elizabeth Carrington, Feb. 24, 1822, typescript in Cabbell-Carrington Collection (Manuscripts Division, University of Virginia Library).

29. Faux, *Memorable Days in America,* p. 51; Wirt to Carrington, Feb. 24, 1822, Cabbell-Carrington Collection.

30. O'Fallon to Calhoun, April 9, 1822, SW LR.

31. O'Fallon to Calhoun, July 1, 1822, *ibid.*

32. *Washington Gazette,* March 4, 1822.

33. "Additions and Donations to the Columbian Museum since its commencement in this City," *Washington National Intelligencer,* April 7, 1824; McKenney to James V. S. Ryley, April 18, 1825, IA LS, vol. 1, p. 451.

34. McKenney to School Superintendents, May 22, 1824, IA LS, vol. 1, p. 80; McKenney to Ryley, April 18, 1825, *ibid.,* p. 451.

35. Second Auditor's Accounts (first series), No. 14418, RG 217, WNRC; McKenney, *Sketches of a Tour to the Lakes,* pp. 412, 201, 240, 243, 248, 299, 313, 314, 315, 393, 429.

36. McKenney to Lewis, Nov. 22, 1820, IT LS, vol. F, p. 79; McKenney to Samuel S. Conant, Jan. 5, 1828, IA LS, vol. 1, p. 284.

37. McKenney to School Superintendents, Aug. 9, 1824, IA LS, vol. 1, p. 173.

38. McKenney to Davis and Force, April 28, 1825, *ibid.,* p. 472.

39. Nicholas Biddle to Daniel Webster, March 2, 1841, SW LR, M-1841.

40. Second Auditor's Accounts (first series), Nos. 5810, 8106, 9570, 9953, 10509, 11679, 10210, 11901, RG 217, WNRC.

41. Hodge, *Indian Tribes of North America,* I: 287-88.

42. Samuel Flagg Bemis, *John Quincy Adams and the Union* (New York, 1956), pp. 80-81.

43. McKenney to John Ridge, Dec. 14, 1828, IA LS, vol. 2, p. 309.

44. Pushmataha quoted in Charles Lanman, *Recollections of Curious Characters and Pleasant Places* (Edinburgh, 1881), pp. 211-12.

45. Hodge, *Indian Tribes of North America,* I: 70.

46. Second Auditor's Accounts (first series), Nos. 8412, 8373, RG 217, WNRC.

47. Lewis Cass to Calhoun, Dec. 15, 1824, IA LR, Michigan Superintendency; McKenney to Cass, Jan. 11, 1825, IA LS, vol. 1, p. 298; McKenney to William P. Duval, Feb. 21, 1825, *ibid.,* p. 361.

48. "Petition of J. O. Lewis, praying compensation for painting the portraits of a number of Indian Chiefs by the direction of the Superintendent of Indian Affairs," Jan. 12, 1841, SEN26A-G7, Records of the United States Senate, RG 46, NA.

49. McKenney to Clark, May 3, 1827, IA LS, vol. 4, p. 45.

50. McKenney to "a Friend," May 15, 1828, printed in *Alexandria Gazette,* May 22, 1828, and *Washington National Intelligencer,* May 31, 1828.

51. "On Retrenchment," May 15, 1828, *House Report* No. 259, 20 Cong., 1 Sess. (Serial 179), p. 187.

52. *Niles' Weekly Register,* June 18, 1831.

53. McKenney to Peter B. Porter, Nov. 3, 1828, IA LS, vol. 5, p. 169; McKenney to Porter, Dec. 9, 1828, IA LR, Miscellaneous; Caleb Atwater, *The Indians of the Northwest, Their Manners, Customs, &c. &c. or Remarks Made on a Tour to Prairie du Chien and Thence to Washington City in 1829* (Columbus, Ohio, 1850), p. 119.

54. King to McKenney, Feb. n.d., 1829, and May 16, 1829, IA LR, Miscellaneous; the draft of McKenney's response is jotted on the May 16 letter.

55. Margaret Bayard Smith, *The First Forty Years of Washington Society,* ed. by Gaillard Hunt (New York, 1906), p. 245.

56. "Expenses of Winnebago Deputation—to Accompany Bill HR458," *House Doc.* No. 129, 20 Cong., 2 Sess. (Serial 186), pp. 4-5.

57. Second Auditor's Accounts (first series), No. 14418, RG 217, WNRC.

58. Frances Trollope, *Domestic Manners of the Americans* (London, 1832), I: 314-15.

59. Jonathan Elliot, *Historical Sketches of the Ten Mile Square Forming the District of Columbia; with a Picture of Washington, Describing Objects of General Interest or Curiosity at the Metropolis of the Union* (Washington, D.C., 1830), pp. 167-68.

60. McKenney to Sparks, Oct. 26, 1829, Sparks Papers.

61. McKenney to John Eaton, March 19, 1830, IA LR, Miscellaneous (Eaton replied on the same letter); McKinney to Charles Bird King, April 3, 1830, Miscellaneous Manuscripts (New-York Historical Society).

62. McKenney to Lewis Clephane and John Gardiner, April 26, 1830, IA LS, vol. 6, p. 393.

63. Clephane and Gardiner to Andrew Jackson, May 7, 1830, IA LR, Miscellaneous.

64. The Mahaskah (White Cloud) lithograph is in the custody of the Library Company of Philadelphia.

65. McKenney to John Quincy Adams, Sept. 7, 1831, and Adams to McKenney, Sept. 12, 1831, Adams Family Papers (Massachusetts Historical Society).

66. McKenney to Adams, Oct. 25 and Dec. 2, 1831, *ibid.*

67. McKenney to Albert Gallatin, Dec. 18, 1831, Albert Gallatin Papers (New-York Historical Society).

68. McKenney to Adams, Jan. 9, 1832, Adams Family Papers.

69. McKenney to Nicholas Biddle, May 19, 1932 (Manuscripts Division, University of Virginia Library).

70. McKenney to Sparks, April 11 and 20, 1833, Sparks Papers.

71. McKenney to Sparks, April 20, 1833, *ibid.*

72. McKenney to Sparks, May 7, 1833, *ibid.*

73. Elbert Herring to John H. Kinzie, John Dougherty, P. L. Chouteau, Pierre Menard, June 1, 1833, IA LS, vol. 10, pp. 394-95.

74. McKenney to Herring, Oct. 21, 1833, Dec. 24, 1835, and Jan. 28, 1836, IA LR, Miscellaneous.

75. Schoolcraft quoted in Donaldson, *The George Catlin Indian Gallery,* p. 801.

76. James Hall to George Catlin, Feb. 12, 1836, printed *ibid.,* pp. 766-67.

77. David Donald, "The Autobiography of James Hall, Western Literary Pioneer," *The Ohio State Archaeological and Historical Quarterly* LVI (1947): 301-02.

78. McKenney to Lehman and Duval, July 20, 1836, Coryell Papers, vol. 3, p. 31 (Historical Society of Pennsylvania).

79. Edward C. Biddle, comp., *Recommendatory Notices of the Indian History and Biography, now Publishing by Edward C. Biddle, Philadelphia: with a List of Subscribers, To March 1, 1837* (Philadelphia, 1837), pp. 10, 14, 16.

80. McKenney to Sparks, May 11, 1838, Sparks Papers.

81. Nicholas B. Wainwright, *Philadelphia in the Romantic Age of Lithography* (Philadelphia, 1958), p. 50.

82. McKenney to Walter Forward, Nov. 3, 1841, Simon Gratz Collection (Historical Society of Pennsylvania).

83. Edward C. Biddle to McKenney, April 24, 1841, SW LR, M-1841.

84. Donald, "Autobiography of James Hall," p. 302.

85. *Philadelphia American Saturday Courier,* Jan. 4, 1840.

86. Donald, "Autobiography of James Hall," p. 302; *Philadelphia American Saturday Courier,* April 2, 1842.

87. King to [Commissioner of Indian Affairs], Feb. 18, 1831, Register of Letters Received, vol. 3, p. 241, RG 75, NA.

88. Samuel C. Stambaugh to Jackson, Sept. 8, 1830, IA LR, Green Bay Agency; Charles J. Kappler, comp. and ed., *Indian Affairs: Laws and Treaties,* vol 2, *Treaties* (Washington, D.C., 1904), pp. 320, 323.

89. For a delightful and fuller discussion of the adventures of The Light and his companions, see John C. Ewers, "When the Light Shone in Washington," *Indian Life on the Upper Missouri* (Norman, Okla., 1968), pp. 75-90.

90. *Ibid.,* p. 76.

91. *Ibid.,* p. 84.

92. Donaldson, *The George Catlin Indian Gallery*, p. 795.

93. McKenney to Sparks, April 20, 1833, Sparks Papers; McKenney to Herring, Sept. 5, 1833, IA LR, Miscellaneous.

94. Nathan Sargent to Cass, May 31, 1833, IA LR, Miscellaneous; Herring to John Garland, June 3, 1833, IA LS, vol. 10, p. 400; Herring to McKenney, *ibid.*, p. 401.

95. Quoted in William T. Hagen, *The Sac and Fox Indians* (Norman, Okla., 1958), p. 215.

96. *Washington National Intelligencer*, Sept. 18, 1837.

97. *Alexandria Gazette*, Oct. 6, 1837.

98. *Washington National Intelligencer*, Oct. 11, 1837.

99. McCloud Manuscript, "About *Indian* visit," n.d., Columbia Historical Society.

100. Hodge, *Indian Tribes of North America*, II: 142-43.

101. *Washington National Intelligencer*, Oct. 6, 1837.

102. *Ibid.*, October 4, 1837.

103. *Ibid.*, Sept. 29, 1837.

104. Catlin to [Commissioner of Indian Affairs], n.d., Register of Letters Received, vol. 10, 1837, RG 75, NA.

105. Catlin to J. H. Hook, Dec. 20, 1832, Consolidated Files of the Quartermaster General, RG 92, Records of the Office of Quartermaster General, NA.

106. McKenney to Carey Harris, Oct. 30, 1837, IA LR, Miscellaneous.

107. Lawrence Taliaferro to Harris, n.d., IA LR, St. Peters Agency.

108. Second Auditor's Accounts (second series), Nos. 1154 and 1421, RG 217, WNRC.

109. McKenney to Harris, Oct. 30, 1837, IA LR, Miscellaneous.

110. Biddle to Harris, Jan. 24, 1838, *ibid.*

111. Biddle to Harris, July 10 and 17, 1838, *ibid.*

112. T. Hartley Crawford to the First and Second Chiefs of the Penobscot Tribe of Indians, April 15, 1842, IA LS, vol. 32, p. 109.

113. James D. Doty to the secretary of war, Sept. 28, 1841, IA LR, Green Bay Agency.

114. John W. Quinney and John N. Chicks to the president of the United States, Nov. 24, 1841, IA LR, *ibid.*

115. J. J. Abert, Francis Markoe, and A. O. Dayton to John Bell, June 18, 1841, IA LR, Miscellaneous; Bell to Abert, Markoe, and Dayton, June 21, 1841, SW LS, vol. 23, p. 458.

116. David Cooke to Mary Cooke, June 20, 1842, printed in Thomas Forsythe Nelson, "An Old Letter: Some Forgotten History of the City and the Man — Washington," *Records of the Columbia Historical Society*, XIV (1911): 42-43.

117. *A Popular Catalogue of the Extraordinary Curiosities in the National Institute, Arranged in the Building Belonging to the Patent Office* (Washington, 1855), p. 44.

118. *Annual Report of the Board of Regents of the Smithsonian Institution . . . 1858* (Washington, D.C., 1859), pp. 41-42.

119. McKenney to [?], March 20, 1857, copy enclosed with "Memorial of John M. Stanley praying Congress to purchase his gallery of Indian paintings now deposited in the Smithsonian Institution," Committee of the Library, SEN34A-H10, RG 46, NA.

120. Luke Lea to W. Sebastian, Jan. 22, 1853, Report Books of the Bureau of Indian Affairs, vol. VII, pp. 205-06, RG 75, NA.

121. *Annual Report of the Board of Regents of the Smithsonian Institution . . . 1858* (Washington, D.C., 1859), p. 42.

122. William Q. Force Manuscript Diary, Jan. 4, 1858, copy in Peter Force Papers (Manuscript Division, Library of Congress).

123. Macaulay to Hughes, Oct. 2, 1826, printed in *Penrith* [England] *Observer,* Dec. 30, 1924.

124. Kaj Birket-Smith, *Charles B. Kings Indianerportraetter I Nationalmuseet* (Copenhagen, 1942), p. 17. The translation of this booklet was kindly provided by Jorgun Sonne of Denmark.

125. *Washington National Intelligencer,* March 6, 1823.

126. King to McKenney, July 5, 1826, IA LR, Miscellaneous.

127. King to Director, May 24, 1859, Charles Bird King file, Redwood Library and Athenaeum.

128. King to Board of Directors, April 21, 1829, printed in George Champlin Mason, *Annals of the Redwood Library and Athenaeum* (Newport, 1891), p. 133; King to Director, May 24, 1859, King file, Redwood Library and Athenaeum.

129. George G. King to W. C. Cozzens, March 31, 1862, King file, Redwood Library and Athenaeum.

130. *Newport Mercury and Weekly News,* March 22, 1862.

Checklist of Extant Charles Bird King Indian Portraits

The sixty-six paintings listed here are the Charles Bird King portraits of American Indians known to be extant as of March 1976. There are undoubtedly others, and the author hopes that readers of this book will bring them to his attention.

For the sake of uniformity, the spellings of the Indian names have been taken from the Frederick Webb Hodge edition of the McKenney and Hall volumes. Published in Edinburgh in 1933, this three-volume edition, entitled *The Indian Tribes of North America,* is by far the most reliable published to date.

Readers should also note that no attempt has been made to differentiate between the original paintings and the replicas. In many cases this could only be an educated guess. Indeed, in some instances even the dates are open to question. Although King frequently dated his portraits on the back of the canvas, the references are often to the date when he painted the replicas, not when he painted the originals.

Dimensions are in inches; height precedes width.

Amiskquew   The Spoon
Menominee, 1831
oil on panel
17¼ x 13½

Gulf States Paper Corporation, Tuscaloosa, Alabama

Apauly Tustennuggee
Creek, 1825
oil on canvas
25 x 30½

National Collection of Fine Arts, Smithsonian Institution, Washington, D.C.

Jesse Bushyhead
Cherokee, 1828
oil on panel
17½ x 13¾

Cherokee National Historical Society, TSA-LA-GI, Tahlequah, Oklahoma

Chenannoquot
Menominee, 1831
oil on panel
17½ x 13¾

Gulf States Paper Corporation, Tuscaloosa, Alabama

Choncape   Big Kansas
Oto, 1822
oil on panel
16¾ x 13⅞

Danish National Museum, Copenhagen, Denmark

Cosneboin
[after James Otto Lewis]
Chippewa, 1827
oil on panel
17¼ x 13⅞

National Collection of Fine Arts, Smithsonian Institution, Washington, D.C.

Hayne Hudjihini   Eagle of Delight
Oto, 1822
oil on panel

16¾ x 13¾   Danish National Museum, Copenhagen, Denmark

17 x 13¾   Gulf States Paper Corporation, Tuscaloosa, Alabama

17 x 14   Thomas Gilcrease Institute of American History and Art, Tulsa, Oklahoma

17½ x 13¾   White House Collection, Washington, D.C.

Hoowaunneka   Little Elk
Winnebago, 1828
oil on panel
17½ x 13⅜

Peabody Museum, Harvard University, Cambridge, Massachusetts

Jackopa   The Six
[after James Otto Lewis]
Chippewa, 1827
oil on panel
17⅜ x 13⅜

National Collection of Fine Arts, Smithsonian Institution, Washington, D.C.

Keokuk   Watchful Fox
Sac, 1827
oil on panel

16¾ x 14   Danish National Museum, Copenhagen, Denmark

17½ x 13¾   Gulf States Paper Corporation, Tuscaloosa, Alabama

17 x 14   Thomas Gilcrease Institute of American History and Art, Tulsa, Oklahoma

1837   Gulf States Paper Corporation, Tuscaloosa, Alabama
oil on canvas
38½ x 26½

Kitcheewabeshas   The Good Martin   Gulf States Paper Corporation, Tuscaloosa, Alabama
[after James Otto Lewis]
Chippewa, 1827
oil on panel
17⅜ x 13½

Mahaskah   White Cloud
Iowa, 1824
oil on panel
17 x 14

Thomas Gilcrease Institute of American History and Art, Tulsa, Oklahoma

Makataimeshekiakiah   Black Hawk   Gulf States Paper Corporation, Tuscaloosa, Alabama
Sac, 1833
oil on panel
29 x 19¾

Mistippee Benjamin
Creek, 1825
oil on canvas, backed with panel
17¼ x 13¾

unknown private collection, sold by the Redwood Library,
1970

Moanahonga Great Walker
Iowa, 1824
oil on panel
17 x 14

Thomas Gilcrease Institute of American History and Art,
Tulsa, Oklahoma

17½ x 13¾

unknown private collection, sold by the Redwood Library,
1970

Mohongo and child
Osage, 1830
oil on panel
17¼ x 14¼

Thornton I. Boileau, Birmingham, Michigan

Monchousia White Plume
Kansa, 1822
oil on panel

16¾ x 13⅝

Danish National Museum, Copenhagen, Denmark

17½ x 13¾

White House Collection, Washington, D.C.

Nesouaquoit Bear in the
Fork of a Tree
Fox, 1837

oil on panel
30 x 25

Chicago Historical Society, Chicago, Illinois

oil on canvas
35½ x 29½

unknown private collection, sold by the Redwood Library,
1970

No Cush
[attribution doubtful]
oil on millboard
2⁹⁄₁₆ x 2

Yale University Art Gallery, New Haven, Connecticut

Notchimine No Heart
Iowa, 1837
oil on panel
17⅜ x 13¼

National Collection of Fine Arts, Smithsonian Institution,
Washington, D.C.

Ongpatonga Big Elk
Omaha, 1822
oil on panel

17½ x 13¾

Newberry Library, Chicago, Illinois

17 x 14

Thomas Gilcrease Institute of American History and Art,
Tulsa, Oklahoma

Peahmuska The Fox Wending   Gulf States Paper Corporation, Tuscaloosa, Alabama
His Course
Fox, 1824
oil on panel
17¼ x 13¾

Peskelechaco
Pawnee, 1822
oil on panel
16¾ x 13⅝   Danish National Museum, Copenhagen, Denmark
17½ x 13¾   unknown private collection, sold by the Redwood Library,
                                   1970

Petalesharro Generous Chief
Pawnee, 1822
16¾ x 13¾   Danish National Museum, Copenhagen, Denmark
17½ x 13¾   Gulf States Paper Corporation, Tuscaloosa, Alabama
17½ x 13¾   Newberry Library, Chicago, Illinois
17 x 14   Thomas Gilcrease Institute of American History and Art,
                                   Tulsa, Oklahoma
17½ x 13¾   White House Collection, Washington, D.C.

Joseph Porus [Polis]   Thomas Gilcrease Institute of American History and Art,
Penobscot, 1842   Tulsa, Oklahoma
oil on panel
17 x 14

Powasheek   To Dash the Water Off   Gulf States Paper Corporation, Tuscaloosa, Alabama
Fox, 1837
oil on panel
17½ x 13¾

Pushmataha   The Sapling Is   Gulf States Paper Corporation, Tuscaloosa, Alabama
Ready for Him
Choctaw, 1824
oil on panel
17¼ x 13¼

John Quinney   Thomas Gilcrease Institute of American History and Art,
Stockbridge, 1842   Tulsa, Oklahoma
oil on panel
17 x 14

Rantchewaime   Female Flying Pigeon
Iowa, 1824
oil on panel
17½ x 13½   Gulf States Paper Corporation, Tuscaloosa, Alabama
17 x 14   Thomas Gilcrease Institute of American History and Art,
                                   Tulsa, Oklahoma

Red Jacket
Seneca, 1828
oil on panel

17 x 14   Yale University Art Gallery, New Haven, Connecticut

17½ x 13½   Albright-Knox Art Gallery, Buffalo, New York

oil on canvas   Historical Society of Pennsylvania
30 x 25

Sharitarish Wicked Chief
Pawnee, 1822
oil on panel

16¾ x 13⅝   Danish National Museum, Copenhagen, Denmark

17½ x 13¾   White House Collection, Washington, D.C.

Shaumonekusse Prairie Wolf
Oto, 1822
oil on panel

16¾ x 13¾   Danish National Museum, Copenhagen, Denmark

17½ x 13½   Gulf States Paper Corporation, Tuscaloosa, Alabama

oil on canvas   Joslyn Art Museum, Omaha, Nebraska
29½ x 24½

oil on panel   White House Collection, Washington, D.C.
17½ x 13¾

17½ x 13¾   unknown private collection, sold by the
                             Geraldine Rockefeller Dodge estate, 1975

Tagoniscoteyeh Black Fox   duVal Radford, Bedford, Virginia
Cherokee, 1828
oil on panel
17½ x 13¾

Tenskwautawaw The Prophet   Thomas Gilcrease Institute of American History and Art,
Shawnee, 1829   Tulsa, Oklahoma
oil on panel
20½ x 23½

Timpoochee Barnard   Gulf States Paper Corporation, Tuscaloosa, Alabama
Yuchi, 1825
oil on panel
17½ x 13¾

Tulcee Mathla   Lowe Art Commission, University of Miami, Florida
Seminole, 1826
oil on panel
17½ x 13¾

David Vann   Thomas Gilcrease Institute of American History and Art,
Cherokee, 1825   Tulsa, Oklahoma
oil on panel
17 x 14

Wabaunsee Causer of Paleness
Potawatomi, 1835
oil on panel
17½ x 13½

unknown museum collection, sold by the
Redwood Library, 1970

Wakechai Crouching Eagle
Sac, 1824
oil on panel
17½ x 13¾

Gulf States Paper Corporation, Tuscaloosa, Alabama

17½ x 13¾

unknown private collection, sold by Geraldine
Rockefeller Dodge estate, 1975

Wanata The Charger
[after James Otto Lewis]
Sioux, 1826
oil on canvas
38½ x 26½

Gulf States Paper Corporation, Tuscaloosa, Alabama

Wijunjon The Light
Assiniboin, 1832
oil on panel
24 x 19¾

Gulf States Paper Corporation, Tuscaloosa, Alabama

Young Cornplanter
Seneca, 1827
oil on panel
16¾ x 13⅝

Danish National Museum, Copenhagen, Denmark

**Young Omawhaw, War Eagle,
Little Missouri, and Pawnees**
1822
oil on canvas
27 x 35½

National Collection of Fine Arts, Smithsonian Institution,
Washington, D.C.

Catalog of
War Department Indian Gallery

This catalog, which appeared in William J. Rhees's 1859 *Guide to the Smithsonian Institution*, is the only known listing of the War Department gallery.

CATALOGUE OF INDIAN PAINTINGS

BELONGING TO THE

GOVERNMENT COLLECTION

····•————◄◆►————•····

1. STING IOWAY ....
2. SHING-YAW-BA-WUS-SEN, *The Figured Stone* ....
3. MISH-SHA-QUAT, *The Clear Sky*—Chippeway Chief . . .Painted by C. B. King from a drawing by Lewis, 1827.
4. PE-A-JUK—A Chippeway ....(King from Lewis, 1827.)
5.
6. AM-EIQUON, *Wooden Ladle* ....(King from Lewis, 1826.)
7. MO-NEE-KAW, *He who goes under ground* ....
8.
9. TU-GO-NIS-CO-TE-YEH, *Black Fox*—Cherokee Chief ....(King, 1828.)
10. EESH-TAH-HUM-LEAH, *Sleepy Eye*—Sioux Chief, from the band called the Sipsctongs.
11. MOOS-M-OM-O-NEE, *The Walking Iron*—Wah-pee-ton Sioux ....(By S. M. Charles, 1837.)
12. LA-KEE-TOO-ME-RA-SHA, *Little Chief*—Pawnee ....(King, 1837.)
13. WAH-RO-NE-SAH, *The Surrounder*—Otoe ....(King, 1837.)
14. WAH-KE-ON-TAW-KAH, *Big Thunder*—Chief of the Medana Kanton Sioux ....(King, 1837.)
15. HAW-CHE-KE-ONG-GA, *He who kills Osages*—Missouri ....(King, 1837.)
16. O-WAN-ICK-KOH, *Little Elk*—Winnebago ....(A. Ford from Lewis, 1826.)
17.
18. _____, Chippeway Chief ....(King from Lewis, 1827.)
19. GA-DE-GE-WE, *Spotted*—Second Chief of the Chippeways, 54 years old ....(King, 1835.)
20. WAA-KANN-SEE-KAA, *Rattlesnake*—Winnebago ....(Ford from Lewis, 1826.)
21. NAA-GAR-NEP, *The one who sits at the head*—Chippeway Chief ....King from Lewis, 1827.)
22. [See 42.] GENERAL PUSH-MA-TA-HA—Choctaw Chief ....
23. MENAWEE—A great Warrior and Creek Chief ....
    This chief commanded the party that killed Gen. McIntosh, and was one of the few that saved themselves from the defeat at the Horse-shoe, by swimming the river, after being badly wounded in the head.
24. MISTEPE—Yoholo Mico's son, a Creek ....(King's 1825.)
25. NAA-SHE-O-SHUCK, *Roaring Thunder*—Sac of Mississippi, son of Black Hawk ....(King, 1837.)
26. YOOSTO, *Spring Frog* ....
27. YOHOLO-MICO—Creek Chief ....(King, 1825.)
28. _____A Creek warrior ....
29. _____A Chippeway Chief ....(King from Lewis, 1827.)
30. I-AU-BEANE—A Chippeway ....(King from Lewis, 1826.)
31. PAH-GUE-SAH-AH—Son of Tecumseh ....(Shaw.)
32. TAH-COL-A-QUOT—A Sac ....
33. [See 77.] KEOKUK, *Watchful Fox*—Chiocook Sac ....
34. PAW-A-SHICK, *To dash the water off*—A Fox Chief ....(Cooke, 1837.)
35. COL. JOHN STEDMAN or STIDHAM ....(King, 1825.)
36. WEA-MATLA—Seminole War Chief ....(King, 1826.)
37. KEE-SHESWA, *The Sun*—Fox warrior ....(King.)
38. TAH-RO-HOU, *Plenty of meat*—Ioway ....(King, 1837.)

Gallery of Art in the Smithsonian building, from the 1859 catalog. Smithsonian Institution Archives.

Bibliography

Records in the National Archives

Record Group 46. Records of the United States Senate.

Record Group 75. Records of the Bureau of Indian Affairs. Records of the Office of Indian Trade.

Record Group 92. Records of the Office of Quartermaster General.

Record Group 107. Records of the Office of the Secretary of War.

Record Group 217. Records of the General Accounting Office.

Manuscripts

Adams Family Papers (microfilm edition). Massachusetts Historical Society.

Cabbell-Carrington Collection. Manuscripts Division, University of Virginia Library.

Lewis S. Coryell Papers. Historical Society of Pennsylvania.

William Q. Force Manuscript Diary (electrostatic copy) in Peter Force Papers. Manuscript Division, Library of Congress.

Albert Gallatin Papers. New-York Historical Society.

Simon Gratz Collection. Historical Society of Pennsylvania.

Charles Bird King File. Redwood Library and Athenaeum.

King Family Papers. Bayard LeRoy King, Saunderstown, R.I.

Thomas L. McKenney letter. Manuscripts Division, University of Virginia Library.

Thomas L. McKenney letters. Miscellaneous Papers, New-York Historical Society.

Albert Newsam Folder. Library Company of Philadelphia, Historical Society of Pennsylvania.

Jared Sparks Papers. Houghton Library, Harvard University.

Subscription book for *History of the Indian Tribes of North America.* Manuscript Division, New York Public Library.

Government Publications

Annual Report of the Board of Regents of the Smithsonian Institution . . . 1858. Washington, D.C., 1859.

Carter, Clarence E., ed. *The Territorial Papers of the United States.* 26 vols. Washington, D.C., 1934-62.

"Expenses of Winnebago Deputation—to Accompany Bill HR458." *House Doc.* No. 129, 20th Cong., 2d Sess. (Serial 186).

Kappler, Charles J., comp. and ed. *Indian Affairs: Laws and Treaties.* Vol. 2, *Treaties.* Washington, D.C., 1904.

"On Retrenchment." May 15, 1828. *House Report* No. 259, 20th Cong., 1st Sess. (Serial 179).

Published Contemporary Works

Atwater, Caleb. *The Indians of the Northwest, Their Manners, Customs, &c. &c. or Remarks Made on a Tour to Prairie Du Chien and Thence to Washington City in 1829.* Columbus, Ohio, 1850.

Biddle, Edward C., comp. *Recommendatory Notices of the Indian History and Biography, now Publishing by Edward C. Biddle, Philadelphia: with a List of Subscribers, To March 1, 1837.* Philadelphia, 1837.

Elliot, Jonathan. *Historical Sketches of the Ten Miles Square Forming the District of Columbia; with a Picture of Washington, Describing Objects of General Interest or Curiosity at the Metropolis of the Union.* Washington, D.C., 1830.

Faux, William. *Memorable Days in America: Being a Journal of a Tour to the United States, Principally Undertaken to Ascertain, by Positive Evidence the Condition and Probable Prospects of British Emigrants; Including Accounts of Mr. Birbeck's Settlement in the Illinois: and Intended to Shew Men and Things as they are in America* (London, 1823). Reprinted in Reuben Gold Thwaites, ed., *Early Western Travels, 1748-1846.* Cleveland, 1905. Vols. VI, XII.

Lanman, Charles. *Recollections of Curious Characters and Pleasant Places.* Edinburgh, 1881.

Lewis, James Otto. *Aboriginal Port-Folio.* Philadelphia, 1835.

Mason, George Champlin. *Annals of the Redwood Library and Athenaeum.* Newport, R.I., 1891.

McKenney, Thomas L. *Sketches of a Tour to the Lakes, of the Character and Customs of the Chippeway Indians, and of Incidents Connected with the Treaty of Fond Du Lac.* Baltimore, 1827.

McKenney, Thomas L., and Hall, James. *History of the Indian Tribes of North America, with Biographical Sketches and Anecdotes of the Principal Chiefs. Embellished with One Hundred and Twenty Portraits, from the Indian Gallery in the Department of War, at Washington.* 3 vols. Philadelphia, 1836-44.

_____. *The Indian Tribes of North America with Biographical Sketches and Anecdotes of the Principal Chiefs.* Frederick Webb Hodge, ed. 3 vols. Edinburgh, 1933.

Nelson, Thomas Forsythe. "An Old Letter: Some Forgotten History of the City and the Man —Washington," *Records of the Columbia Historical Society* XIV (1911): 25-48.

Poore, Benjamin Perley. *Perley's Reminiscences.* 2 vols. Philadelphia, 1886.

A Popular Catalogue of the Extraordinary Curiosities in the National Institute, Arranged in the Building Belonging to the Patent Office. Washington, D.C., 1855.

Rhees, William Jones. *An Account of the Smithsonian Institution, Its Founder, Building, Operations, Etc., Prepared from the Reports of Prof. Henry to the Regents, and Other Authentic Sources.* Washington, D.C., 1859.

Smith, Margaret Bayard. *The First Forty Years of Washington Society.* Gaillard Hunt, ed. New York, 1906.

Trollope, Frances. *Domestic Manners of the Americans.* 2 vols. London, 1832.

Newspapers

Alexandria Gazette

Newport Mercury and Weekly News

Niles' Weekly Register

Penrith [England] Observer

Philadelphia American Saturday Courier

Philadelphia Franklin Gazette

Washington Daily National Intelligencer

Washington Gazette

Books and Articles

Bemis, Samuel Flagg. *John Quincy Adams and the Union.* New York, 1956.

Birket-Smith, Kaj. *Charles B. Kings Indianerportraetter I Nationalmuseet.* Copenhagen, 1942.

Cosentino, Andrew J. "Charles Bird King: An Appreciation." *The American Art Journal* VI (May 1974): 54-71.

Donald, David. "The Autobiography of James Hall, Western Literary Pioneer." *Ohio State Archaeological and Historical Quarterly* LVI (1947): 295-304.

Donaldson, Thomas. *The George Catlin Indian Gallery in the U.S. National Museum (Smithsonian Institution), with Memoir and Statistics.* Washington, D.C., 1887.

Ewers, John C. "Charles Bird King, Painter of Indian Visitors to the Nation's Capital." *Annual Report of the Board of Regents of the Smithsonian Institution.* Washington, D.C., 1954.

————. *Indian Life on the Upper Missouri.* Norman, Okla., 1968.

Hagen, William T. *The Sac and Fox Indians.* Norman, Okla., 1958.

Hodge, Frederick Webb. "The Origin and Destruction of a National Indian Portrait Gallery." *Holmes Anniversary Volume.* Washington, D.C., 1916.

Kinietz, W. Vernon. *John Mix Stanley and His Indian Paintings.* Ann Arbor, Mich., 1942.

Prucha, Francis Paul. *Indian Peace Medals in American History.* Madison, Wis., 1971.

Viola, Herman J. "Invitation to Washington." *American West* IX (January 1972): 18-31.

————. "Portraits, Presents, and Peace Medals: Thomas L. McKenney and the Indian Visitors to Washington." *American Scene* XI (June 1970).

————. *Thomas L. McKenney, Architect of America's Early Indian Policy, 1816-1830.* Chicago, 1974.

————. "Washington's First Museum: The Indian Office Collection of Thomas L. McKenney." *Smithsonian Journal of History* III (Fall 1968): 1-18.

Wainwright, Nicholas B. *Philadelphia in the Romantic Age of Lithography.* Philadelphia, 1958.

Index